I0408109

DEPARTMENT OF THE NAVY

GENERAL POLICY FOR THE INACTIVATION, RETIREMENT, AND DISPOSITION OF U.S. NAVAL VESSELS

OPNAVINST 4770.5H
N9
24 Apr 2014

OPNAV INSTRUCTION 4770.5H

From: Chief of Naval Operations

Subj: INACTIVATION, RETIREMENT, AND DISPOSITION OF U.S. NAVAL
       VESSELS

Ref: (a) OPNAVINST 4780.6E
       (b) 10 U.S.C.
       (c) OPNAVINST 5090.1D
       (d) Naval Ships Technical Manual
       (e) OPNAVINST 1541.5
       (f) OPNAVINST 4730.5Q
       (g) OPNAVINST 4730.7F
       (h) OPNAVINST 5400.44A
       (i) SECNAVINST 4900.50A
       (j) NWP 1-03.1
       (k) OPNAVINST 4440.19F
       (l) SECNAVINST 5030.8B

1. Purpose. To set forth the policy and guidance for the
inactivation, transfer, and disposal of vessels of the U.S. Navy
and the administration of those assets following inactivation.
This instruction has been revised substantially and should be
reviewed in its entirety.

    a. Establishes a new chapter (chapter 6) concerning foreign
military transfers and excess defense article ships and the
removal of installed systems and equipment from ships designated
for foreign military sales (FMS).

    b. Revises action required to retire a ship prior to its
expected service life (except Military Sealift Command (MSC)
vessels), revises action required to extend a ship's expected
service life (ESL), and updates MSC requirements for
notification of the retirement of an MSC vessel to the Chief of
Naval Operations (CNO).

    c. Provides a new ship inactivation timeline for
conventional ships that highlights specific periods, events, and
decision points critical in the execution of ship inactivations
and FMS transfers.

2. <u>Cancellation</u>. OPNAVINST 4770.5G.

3. <u>Background</u>. Inactive vessels designated as retention assets form a reserve of sea power available for future reactivation. It is the Navy's objective to maintain retention assets in a fixed state of preservation consistent with available funds. It is further the Navy's objective to maintain all inactive vessels, whether for retention or pending disposal, in compliance with applicable Federal, State, and local environmental laws and regulations. Throughout this instruction, the term "vessel" refers to all naval ships and service craft listed in the Naval Vessel Register. Additional guidance specific to the retirement and disposal of service craft and other non-Naval Vessel Register vessels can be found per reference (a).

   a. Inactive vessels designated for retention shall be maintained in the highest practicable state of preservation that is consistent with their inactive status, available funds, and higher priority Navy requirements for material as determined by the CNO. Deputy Chief of Naval Operations (DCNO), Warfare Systems (CNO N9) shall review the composition of the inventory of inactive ships and their material condition to determine the number of vessels to be held as retention assets, as well as identify which vessels will be sold, leased, donated, or disposed of as part of the ship disposition process.

   b. Nuclear-powered ships and submarines are de-fueled during the inactivation process. These vessels, having no further useful life, are not relied on as a reserve of sea power.

   c. Inactivation, storage, maintenance, and preparation for disposal of Navy vessels must comply with applicable Federal, State, and local laws and regulations. References (b) through (g) provide policy and guidance for matters concerning environmental protection compliance that shall be stringently adhered to with the implementation of this instruction.

4. <u>Scope</u>

   a. This instruction applies to all conventionally-powered and non-self-propelled vessels of the U.S. Navy that are listed in the Naval Vessel Register.

b. This instruction also applies to the inactivation and disposal of nuclear-powered ships and submarines; ships and service craft with nuclear support spaces; and nuclear engineering and nuclear support facilities as governed by instructions implemented by the Commander, Naval Sea Systems Command (COMNAVSEASYSCOM). This instruction does not supersede or change responsibilities and authorities of the Director, Naval Nuclear Propulsion Program (N00N), as outlined in Executive Order 12344, which is codified by section 7158 of title 41, United States Code (U.S.C.) and section 2406 of title 50, U.S.C.

5. Action. Addressees are responsible for implementing and administering the policies and guidance found herein. COMNAVSEASYSCOM is the Navy's agent in matters pertaining to the inactivation, maintenance, storage, and disposal of naval vessels and will issue additional procedures as necessary to ensure the uniform compliance with the policies herein. COMNAVSEASYSCOM is also the implementing agent for foreign military transfers. The major stakeholders' roles and responsibilities are outlined per chapter 1.

6. Definitions and Acronyms. Appendix A defines terms and acronyms used in this instruction

7. Records Management. Records created as a result of this instruction, regardless of media and format, shall be managed per the Secretary of the Navy (SECNAV) Manual 5210.1 of January 2012.

8. Forms and Reports

a. OPNAV 5400/1, Navy Organization Change Request, is available for download from Naval Forms Online at https://navalforms.documentservices.dla.mil.

b. OPNAV 4790/CK, Ship's Configuration Change Form, is available for download from Naval Forms Online at https://navalforms.documentservices.dla.mil.

c. DD Form 1149, Requisition and Invoice/Shipping Document, is available for download from the Department of Defense (DoD) Forms Management Web site at http://www.dtic.mil/whs/directives/infomgt/forms/eforms/dd1149.pdf and the Defense Contract Management Agency at www.dcma.mil/dcman/NPP/files/dd1149.pdf.

    d. The reports required by this instruction are exempt from reports control by SECNAV Manual 5214.1, section IV, paragraph 71.

J. P. AU
Deputy Chief of Naval
Operations, Warfare Systems

Distribution:
Electronic only, via Department of the Navy Issuances Web site
http://doni.documentservices.dla.mil

TABLE OF CONTENTS

CHAPTER 1
ROLES AND RESPONSIBILITIES

1. <u>General</u>. This chapter identifies the roles and responsibilities of the major stakeholders involved with the retirement, transfer, disposition, and disposal of U.S. naval vessels.

2. <u>CNO</u>

a. <u>Director, Warfare Integration (OPNAV N9I)</u> shall:

(1) Provide ship inactivation and disposition policy guidance.

(2) Serve as the requirements and resource sponsor for the maintenance, disposition, and disposal of ships in the inactive ship inventory. Maintain oversight of the ship inactivation funding account throughout the Planning, Programming, Budgeting, and Execution (PPBE) process. After the first year of lay-up in the inactive fleet, fund the inactive ship and facility maintenance costs for vessels in the inactive inventory.

(3) Manage the ship inactivation and disposition decision process which includes chairing the Ship Inactivation Decision (SID) and Ship Disposition Review (SDR) conferences, and provide all information, including status changes, to those vessels already in the inactive ship inventory to the CNO for approval.

(4) Assign disposition categories for all ships scheduled for retirement, including those vessels designated to support fleet training requirements, experimental use, and those being disposed of via donation, interagency or foreign military transfer, artificial reefing, and dismantling.

(5) Pursuant to section 7308 of reference (b), initiate correspondence to SECNAV, via CNO, recommending specific vessels be stricken from the Naval Vessel Register prior to their disposal.

(6) Coordinate decisions regarding changes in the method of disposal once a vessel is stricken from the Naval Vessel Register.

(7) Coordinate with the respective Office of the Chief of Naval Operations (OPNAV) ship resource and platform sponsors; Commander, U.S. Pacific Fleet (COMPACFLT); Commander, U.S. Fleet Forces Command (COMUSFLTFORCOM); fleet type commanders (TYCOM); COMNAVSEASYSCOM; ship program managers; and the Board of Inspection and Survey (INSURV) on fleet requests to waive inactivation surveys as described in chapter 10.

b. <u>OPNAV Ship Resource and Platform Sponsors</u>. Director, Strategic Mobility and Combat Logistics (OPNAV N42); DCNO, Information Dominance (CNO N2/N6); Director, Innovation, Technology, and Requirements (OPNAV N84/Office of Naval Research (ONR)); Director, Expeditionary Warfare (OPNAV N95); Director, Surface Warfare (OPNAV N96); Director, Undersea Warfare (OPNAV N97); and Director, Air Warfare (OPNAV N98) shall:

(1) Support the ship inactivation and disposition decision process via the SID and SDR conferences.

(2) Provide OPNAV N9I with the Future Years Defense Program's (FYDP) retirement schedule and determine future mobilization requirements.

(3) Budget and program funds through the PPBE process for the planning and execution of the nuclear-powered ships' inactivation, disposal, and recycling program to support the inactivation of ships scheduled across the FYDP.

(4) Budget and program funds through the PPBE process for the inactivation of non-nuclear ships and costs associated with the first year's maintenance in the inactive ship inventory. Provide OPNAV N9I with funding profiles for ships that are scheduled to be inactivated across the FYDP throughout the PPBE process.

(5) Assist in the reprogramming of funds necessary to execute the inactivation of a ship when retirement date is accelerated and does not allow program objective memorandum (POM) programming or when planned FMS hot ship transfers become non-executable.

(6) Coordinate with COMNAVSEASYSCOM and the MSC ship program managers and life cycle managers for modernization planning and execution requirements to mobilize assets.

(7) Coordinate with OPNAV N9I and COMNAVSEASYSCOM when directing a hot ship transfer of a retiring vessel to another DoD Service, Federal, State, or local government or non-government agency.

(8) Coordinate and fund the removal of non-transferable technology prior to transfer to foreign military.

(9) Fund the first year of lay-up in storage costs for inactive ship and facility maintenance for defueled formerly nuclear-powered ships and submarine tenders.

(10) Coordinate manning level requirements for ships scheduled to inactivate with the ship's chain of command.

(11) Provide for Electronic Charting Display Information System-Navy (ECDIS-N) or navigational charts and publications to reactivated ships and service crafts.

c. DCNO for Manpower, Personnel, Training, and Education (CNO N1)/Chief of Naval Personnel shall:

(1) Support the ship inactivation and disposition decision process via the SID conference.

(2) Coordinate manning level requirements for ships scheduled to inactivate with the ship's commanding officer (CO), in coordination with the appropriate TYCOM and ship resource sponsors.

(3) Provide updates to training policy contained in chapter 14.

d. Director, Organization and Management Branch (DNS-33) shall:

(1) Support the ship inactivation and disposition decision process via the SID conference.

(2) Per reference (h), staff OPNAV 5400/1 Navy Organization Change Request to the appropriate OPNAV ship resource and platform sponsor; DCNO, Fleet Readiness and Logistics (CNO N4); CNO N2/N6; DCNO, Integration of Resources and Capabilities (CNO N8); CNO N9; and OPNAV N9I; as well as CNO N1; DCNO, Operations, Plans and Strategy (CNO N3/N5); Director, Fleet Readiness (OPNAV N43); Director, Shore Readiness (OPNAV N46); Director, Programming Division (OPNAV N80); and Director, Financial Management and Budget Division (OPNAV N82) to support the inactivation of a nuclear-powered vessel (to include related homeport changes, planned inactivation fiscal year (FY)) and projected decommissioning dates.

e. <u>Director, Navy History and Heritage Command (DNS-H)</u> shall:

(1) Support the ship inactivation and disposition decision process via the SID and SDR conferences, including development of determinations of eligibility (or determinations of ineligibility) for listing on the national register of historic places as required for National Historic Preservation Act compliance.

(2) Perform a curator survey on ships that are scheduled to inactivate within 12 months prior to the date of their retirement.

(3) Collect, preserve, and exhibit naval relics, trophies, paintings, and other memorabilia of historical significance from inactivating vessels.

(4) Coordinate the removal of designated items as described in chapter 11.

(5) Coordinate the submission and disposition of the vessel's final command history and historical records (including command operation reports, war diaries, and deck logs) to OPNAV DNS-H Naval Warfare Division, Ships Histories Branch, and TYCOM with the responsible vessel custodian.

f. <u>OPNAV N43</u> shall:

(1) Support the ship inactivation and disposition decision process via the SID and SDR conferences.

(2) Authorize the use of environmentally-remediated vessels in a fleet training exercise per reference (c).

(3) Validate all fleet requests for vessels used in support of fleet training exercises.

(4) Coordinate environmental preparations on ships designated for use in fleet training exercises, as funded by the requestor.

g. Director, Energy and Environmental Readiness (OPNAV N45) shall:

(1) Support the ship inactivation and disposition decision process via the SID and SDR conferences.

(2) Coordinate all actions (described in chapter 5) for any vessel used in support of fleet training exercises, reefing, experimental use, live fire test and evaluation or weapons effect testing, or other disposition with potential for direct impact to the marine environment.

h. OPNAV N46 shall:

(1) Perform duties as OPNAV resource sponsor for service craft program.

(2) Assess COMNAVSEASYSCOM requests to strike service craft from the Naval Vessel Register and forward such requests to the Assistant Secretary of the Navy for Research, Development, and Acquisition (ASN (RD&A)).

i. Director, International Engagement Division (OPNAV N52) shall:

(1) Support the ship disposition decision process via the SDR conference.

(2) Provide OPNAV N9I with foreign transfer requirement projections.

(3) Coordinate ship transfer plans with Navy International Programs Office (IPO), OPNAV N9I, COMNAVSEASYSCOM, and the fleet.

(4) Coordinate with the Navy IPO to advise OPNAV N9I when international partners no longer have viable interest in vessels that are on hold for foreign ship transfer.

3. <u>President, INSURV (OPNAV N09P)</u> shall:

a. Support the ship inactivation and disposition decision process via the SID and SDR conferences.

b. Conduct a survey on vessels that are scheduled to inactivate and be retained in an out of commission, in reserve (OCIR) or out of service, in reserve (OSIR) status. Coordinate with OPNAV N9I, COMNAVSEASYSCOM, and TYCOM on de-scoping inactivation survey requirements when applicable for specific vessels.

c. Coordinate with COMNAVSEASYSCOM and TYCOM on requirements for conducting surveys on vessels designated for hot ship transfer within 18 months prior to the planned retirement date.

d. Coordinate with COMNAVSEASYSCOM on requirements for conducting surveys on vessels designated for cold ship transfer.

e. Conduct surveys on inactive ships as needed.

f. Conduct surveys on service craft per reference (a).

4. <u>COMNAVSEASYSCOM</u> shall:

a. Be the implementing agent for foreign military transfers and issues guidance to TYCOM on the removal of non-transferrable technology.

b. Support the ship inactivation and disposition decision process via the SID and SDR conferences.

c. Disseminate additional procedures to comply with the policies and guidelines herein and to aid in ensuring compliance by claimant activities.

d.   Perform command and support responsibilities assigned to the COMNAVSEASYSCOM Inactive Ships Management Office (INACTSHIPOFF) Portsmouth, VA, and the COMNAVSEASYSCOM Inactive Ships On-site Maintenance Office (INACTSHIPMAINTO).

e.   Provide for the custody, security, maintenance, and readiness of vessels under COMNAVSEASYSCOM INACTSHIPOFF, and formerly nuclear-powered ships and submarines, and vessels with nuclear support facilities (e.g., submarine tenders), that are berthed at a naval shipyard and are the responsibility of that yard.

f.   Develop and disseminate a ship inactivation plan per the OPNAV assigned ship disposition within 6 months of the ship's retirement

g.   Provide execution funding as programmed by the OPNAV ship resource and platform sponsors to support inactivation work to be completed by the fleet and COMNAVSEASYSCOM INACTSHIPMAINTO.

h.   Accept ships upon arrival at the COMNAVSEASYSCOM INACTSHIPMAINTO that have been prepared for lay-up per reference (d), chapter 050, and the ship's inactivation plan, and maintain oversight over those Navy vessels stored at a reserve facility.

i.   When authorized, prepare vessels that are in the inactive ships inventory for final disposal.

j.   Manage and execute the disposal of vessels, including the requirement for compliance with the National Historic Preservation Act.

k.   Implement the foreign transfers of inactive service craft under COMNAVSEASYSCOM custody per reference (i).

l.   Execute the FMS program as directed by the Navy IPO. Provide additional instructions to COMUSFLTFORCOM and COMPACFLT, in coordination with OPNAV N9I, regarding the preparation of ships for foreign military transfer.

m.   Coordinate with INSURV on requirements for surveys on vessels authorized for hot ship transfer within 18 months prior to the planned retirement date.

n. Coordinate case funding for the execution of FMS requirements (i.e., funding for any alterations or improvements, ship transfer support, inactive equipment maintenance, vessel storage, and preservation requirements) and advise OPNAV N9I when the FMS case is established.

o. Coordinate with OPNAV N9I before authorizing the removal of installed equipment from assets that are designated for FMS.

p. Specify the payback requirements when responding to cannibalization requests. In the case of donation hold assets, COMNAVSEASYSCOM shall retain approval authority for asset removal and payback requirements.

q. Provide program and budget requirements to OPNAV N9I for the inactivation, maintenance, and disposal of naval vessels. Provide OPNAV N9I with funding profiles and execution status reports for non-nuclear and nuclear-powered inactive vessels as requested.

r. Execute ship inactivation funds from the OPNAV ship resource and platform sponsors. Coordinate budget preparation and financial administration for all ship inactivations and vessel disposals for which funds have been provided. Provide a detailed summary of all funds expended towards a donated ship from resources provided by the OPNAV resource sponsor for Inactive Ships as part of the annual financial review.

s. Recommend changes to ship disposition assignments to OPNAV N9I as necessary.

t. Submit proposals for inspections of inactive ships that are under COMNAVSEASYSCOM responsibility to OPNAV N09P via OPNAV N9I as necessary pursuant to chapter 10.

u. Initiate correspondence to ASN (RD&A) to strike service craft from the Naval Vessel Register in support of disposal efforts.

v. Certify vessels authorized for use in support of fleet training exercises, live fire test and evaluation, or weapons effectiveness testing have been prepared to environmental standards.

w. Prepare an annual report for submission by OPNAV N45 to the Environmental Protection Agency (EPA) administrator for vessels sunk during Navy fleet training exercises within the preceding calendar year.

x. Coordinate the removal of equipment from retention assets to support COMUSFLTFORCOM and COMPACFLT requirements where payback replacement exceeds 12 months or a waiver of payback is requested and notify OPNAV N9I and OPNAV ship resource and platform sponsor.

y. Ensure vessels being transferred outside of naval custody no longer have the outward appearance of any active Navy vessels by painting out names and numbers of naval vessels and service craft, except for vessels donated for museum or memorial use.

z. Provide ship disposal plan inputs to OPNAV N9I.

aa. In the case of split inactivations, execute operational control (OPCON) and administrative control (ADCON) once the inactivating ship arrives at the final inactivation site and is transferred to COMNAVSEASYSCOM INACTSHIPMAINTO.

ab. Advise OPNAV N9I of Navy's requirement to remove installed systems in appendix B from inactivating vessels to support Navy requirements (e.g., Phalanx close-in weapons system as part of the COMNAVSEASYSCOM inactivation plan.

ac. Liaison with Navy IPO, to identify non-transferable technology on vessels designated for foreign military transfer and issue appropriate guidance via naval message to TYCOM. Additional information can be found in chapter 6.

5. Commander, Navy Supply Systems Command (COMNAVSUPSYSCOM) shall:

a. Support the ship inactivation and disposition decision process via the SDR conference.

b. Act as the program manager for silver service items. Coordinate the custody and preservation of silver service items aboard vessels.

c. Coordinate the removal and disposition of silver service items during the decommissioning and disposal process.

6. <u>COMUSFLTFORCOM and COMPACFLT</u> shall:

a. Support the ship inactivation and disposition decision process via the SID and SDR conferences.

b. Issue implementing directives as necessary and ensure compliance by subordinate activities.

c. Coordinate with TYCOM and numbered fleet commanders on inactivation availability period for ships under COMUSFLTFORCOM and COMPACFLT OPCON via the quarterly scheduling conference.

d. In coordination with the TYCOM for nuclear-powered ships, submit an OPNAV 5400/1 per reference (h), providing notification to the Director, Navy Staff (DNS) of the projected decommissioning date to include the planned inactivation availability start date and any change in homeport as a result. Update the OPNAV 5400/1 as required based on changes to the inactivation timeline. Additional guidance provided in chapter 3.

e. In coordination with the TYCOM, for non-nuclear powered ships (excluding MSC vessels), submit an OPNAV 5400/1 per reference (h) guidelines, providing formal notification to DNS on the retirement date for battle force vessels. Since MSC ships are manned by civilian mariners and are not assigned homeports, an OPNAV 5400/1 is not required to inactivate United States Naval Ships (USNS) assigned to MSC.

f. COs, masters, and officers in charge for all ships shall submit a naval message announcing the ship's official retirement date - normally transmitted in conjunction with the decommissioning or out of service ceremony. This message shall be addressed "TO" the chain of command and "INFO" (for "information") all appropriate support activities, including the CNO (N00), CNO N8, CNO N9, OPNAV N9I, DNS-H, Naval Vessel Register, COMNAVSEASYSCOM Surface Warfare Directorate (NAVSEA 21), and COMNAVSEASYSCOM Naval Systems Engineering Directorate, Cost Engineering and Industrial Analysis Division (NAVSEA 05C) and shall include a brief history of the significant events in the life of the ship.

g. Execute OPCON and ADCON of a ship that is scheduled for inactivation and safe stowage until the ship has been delivered to COMNAVSEASYSCOM's custody at the COMNAVSEASYSCOM INACTSHIPMAINTO.

h. In the case of split inactivations, execute OPCON and ADCON until the inactivating ship arrives at the final inactivation site and is transferred to COMNAVSEASYSCOM INACTSHIPMAINTO.

i. Oversee the planning and execution of ship inactivations. Provide and fund barge support for duty crew messing and berthing during inactivation availabilities. Provide funding for intra-service supply support operations team and offload of ship's spare parts during ship inactivation when a ship is to be struck from the Naval Vessel Register. For nuclear ships, coordinate with COMNAVSEASYSCOM as appropriate.

j. Comply with additional COMNAVSEASYSCOM directives for execution of the inactivation process.

k. Coordinate directly with OPNAV N9I prior to altering the inactivation schedule of a ship that is previously designated for hot ship transfer to a foreign country.

l. Act as the implementing agent for foreign hot ship transfers. Maintain responsibility for ships that are designated for hot ship transfer until custody is transferred to the foreign government.

m. Coordinate with COMNAVSEASYSCOM to identify non-transferrable equipment on ships slated for FMS, and to issue corresponding guidance, per the appendix C timeline, on inactivating ships which includes material offload, and stripping of specific hardware and systems.

n. Develop cost estimates, or task regional maintenance centers to develop cost estimates, for inactivation tasks that are considered beyond the capability of ship's force and provide them to COMNAVSEASYSCOM for budget development and funding.

o. Coordinate towing requirements, including the funding of vessel towing per the Navy tow manual to the post-inactivation storage facility.

p.   Coordinate with the Navy curator for removal of designated items as described in chapter 11.

q.   Provide DNS with appropriate documentation when requesting to retire a ship before reaching its ESL as discussed in chapter 2.

r.   Coordinate with OPNAV N9I with appropriate documentation when:

(1) Requesting to extend a ship's ESL as discussed in chapter 2.

(2) Requesting to extend a ship's retirement date beyond the CNO's planned FY.

7.   <u>MSC</u> shall:

a.   Support the ship inactivation and disposition decision process via the SID and SDR conferences.

b.   Coordinate with COMUSFLTFORCOM, COMPACFLT, and respective OPNAV ship resource and platform sponsor to provide OPNAV N9I with the ship inactivation schedule over the FYDP and to determine future mobilization requirements for inactivating ships.

c.   Establish inactivation availability and out-of-service dates in coordination with COMUSFLTFORCOM and COMPACFLT within the approved FY.

d.   Maintain responsibility for MSC ships until transfer of custody to COMNAVSEASYSCOM at a COMNAVSEASYSCOM INACTSHIPMAINTO, or transfer of custody to Maritime Administration (MARAD), as applicable.

e.   Manage the planning and execution of MSC ship inactivations per reference (d), chapter 050, for CNO assigned ship dispositions, and the MARAD reserve fleet manual for ships assigned to MARAD for disposition, in coordination with COMNAVSEASYSCOM.

f. Budget and program funds in coordination with respective OPNAV ship resource and platform sponsor and plan requirements for inactivation (i.e., towing preparations, towing, first-year maintenance costs, and other costs associated with the ship's movement in support of arrival or removal from its storage site).

g. Coordinate with COMUSFLTFORCOM and COMPACFLT on the planned inactivation start date within the CNO approved inactivation FY and the projected out-of-service date. Additional guidance can be found in chapter 3.

h. MSC shall submit a naval message announcing MSC ship inactivation 90 days prior to the actual retirement date. The message must provide the date the vessel will be placed out of service along with the planned disposition. Any outstanding inactivation funding requirements shall be addressed as well. The message shall be "TO" CNO WASHINGTON DC//N00/N09/DNS33/ N3/N5/N9/N9I/N4/N42 (or respective resource sponsor), COMUSFLTFORCOM, COMPACFLT, COMNAVSEASYSCOM WASHINGTON DC/SEA 21/SEA 21I// and COMNAVSEASYSCOM DET INACTSHIPOFF PORTMOUTH VA//00/01//. The message shall align with the SID and SDR recommendations and the 30-year shipbuilding plan (if it is a battle force ship). COMNAVSEASYSCOM will develop the ship's inactivation plan based on the message. MSC shall send a message to COMUSFLTFORCOM or COMPACFLT, info all concerned to request a change to the ship's retirement date. COMUSFLTFORCOM or COMPACFLT shall notify OPNAV N9I of the approved change.

i. MSC shall submit a naval message announcing the official retirement date for all MSC vessels. The message will normally be transmitted in conjunction with the out of service ceremony. The message should be "TO" CNO WASHINGTON DC//N00/N09/DNS33/N3/N5/N9/N9I/N4/N42 (or respective resource sponsor), COMUSFLTFORCOM, and COMPACFLT. It shall "INFO" all appropriate support activities, to include COMNAVSEASYSCOM (NAVSEA 21 and NAVSEA 05C). The message should include a brief history of the significant events in the life of the ship.

8. United States Marine Corps (USMC) shall:

a. Provide input to OPNAV N95 on amphibious ship retirements.

b.   Represent USMC equities as a member of the long range shipbuilding strategy integrated product team.

c.   Represent USMC equities in the ship inactivation and disposition decision process via the SID and SDR conferences.

CHAPTER 2
SHIP RETIREMENT POLICY

1. Policy. SECNAV is the approval authority for the change in status of all active ships of the U.S. Navy (including MSC). Thus, these vessels may not be decommissioned or placed out of service without the direct authorization of SECNAV.

2. General. The Navy continuously evaluates the threat and evolving security environment to determine the necessary forces required. The numbers and types of ships used to balance the Navy's current and future mission requirements are outlined in the Navy's annual long-range plan for construction of naval vessels. This 30-year shipbuilding plan formulates the baseline for decisions concerning which battle force ship types should be retired. The Navy uses a ship's ESL for planning the number of years a battle force ship is expected to remain in service. The process of determining the requirement to retire a ship typically begins with the OPNAV ship resource and platform sponsors (under CNO N2/N6, N4, N8, and N9) presenting their sponsor program proposals during the development of the POM.

3. Ship Retirements. Refers to the decommissioning of a commissioned ship or the placement of a USNS or service craft out-of-service. Transfers between active status and the Navy Reserve Force (NRF) do not constitute a retirement.

4. Decision Factors. At a minimum, the following factors should be considered when determining eligibility for retirement:

    a. Whether the ship has reached its ESL. In general, once a battle force ship reaches its ESL, the ship is expected to retire from active service. However, there are exceptions that result in a ship being retired prior to reaching its ESL or remaining active beyond its ESL (e.g., current and future force structure requirements, mission requirements, budgetary constraints, extraordinary events such as a natural disaster or an accident).

    b. Whether the ship's operational effectiveness and continued interoperability is still viable to mission requirements.

c. Whether required system upgrades and design changes can be feasibly made to justify a ship's continued service.

d. The material fitness of the vessel pursuant to section 7304 of reference (b).

e. Impact on current and expected future force structure (ability to man, maintain and operate active vessels).

5. <u>OPNAV 5400/1</u>. Per reference (h), an OPNAV 5400/1 is required to be submitted in support of each ship (excluding MSC vessels) under COMUSFLTFORCOM or COMPACFLT OPCON and scheduled for inactivation. The purpose of OPNAV 5400/1 is to provide DNS with notification of a ship's inactivation, retirement, or the disestablishment of a military department or attachment aboard a vessel. OPNAV 5400/1 is also required by DNS to support the ship's inactivation process and to update various programmatic databases, including the Standard Naval Distribution List, Total Force Manpower Management System, Global Force Management, Internet Ship Management Information System, Programming and Budget Information System, and the Naval Vessel Register. In addition, OPNAV 5400/1:

a. Provides a comprehensive proposal for CNO or SECNAV staff to review.

b. Provides a means for approval or disapproval to execute the proposed action.

c. Allows for congressional notification of an action prior to public announcement.

6. <u>Action Required to Retire a Ship Prior to ESL</u>. Recommendations for the early retirement of a ship under fleet OPCON (as a result of either the POM process, the ship's material fitness, or an extraordinary event) shall be accompanied by an OPNAV 5400/1 that, at a minimum, addresses the following:

a. Describe why it is in the best interest of the Navy to retire the ship prior to reaching its ESL.

b.   Identify any gaps in capability that will occur upon the retirement of each ship, including the duration of that capability gap.

c.   Recommend strategies to mitigate gaps in capability.

d.   Planned date of retirement and, in the case of a nuclear ship, also identify the start date of the ship's inactivation maintenance availability.

7.   <u>Action Required to Extend a Ship's ESL</u>.   All requests to extend a ship's ESL, if not generated by the applicable resource sponsor, must be formally coordinated with the respective OPNAV ship resource and platform sponsors (CNO N2/N6 and OPNAV N42, N84/ONR, N95, N96, N97, N98) and COMNAVSEASYSCOM.   In addition, coordination is required with OPNAV N9I to assess the impact on battleforce inventory requirements.

8.   <u>Non-Battle Force Ships</u>.   Retirement decisions concerning non-battle force ships shall be coordinated with the fleet operational commander, OPNAV ship resource and platform sponsors, and OPNAV N9I via the SID and SDR process.

9.   <u>Service Craft</u>.   Service craft are not part of the Navy's battle force.   The guidelines for determining and reporting when service craft will be removed from service are contained in reference (a).

CHAPTER 3
INACTIVATION POLICY

1. General. Ships typically begin the inactivation process at the commencement of the inactivation availability. During this period, ships are considered to be in an in commission, in reserve status; exceptions shall be coordinated through the respective OPNAV ship resource and platform sponsor.

a. TYCOM should take necessary precautions to ensure ships designated for foreign military transfer are not stripped of equipment while undergoing their inactivation availability as discussed in chapter 6.

b. The ship's TYCOM is responsible for the inactivation of nuclear vessels and inactivation and retirement of non-nuclear vessels. COMNAVSEASYSCOM shall prepare and issue the plans for inactivation and preservation of vessels, including the adequate control of the quality and progress of inactivation work. Inactivation of nuclear-powered ships and submarines; service craft with nuclear support spaces; and nuclear engineering and nuclear support facility shall be governed by instructions implemented by COMNAVSEASYSCOM.

c. Hulls of nuclear-powered ships, submarines, nuclear-related tenders, and service craft shall be retained in safe storage until the disposal and decontamination availabilities are executed by the assigned naval shipyard as scheduled by COMNAVSEASYSCOM.

d. To the maximum extent possible, the inactivation of the vessel is normally carried out in the ship's homeport.

2. Inactivation Decision. Inactivation decisions are formalized during the SID conference as discussed in chapter 4 and are disseminated as part of the report to congress on the annual long-range plan for construction of naval vessels - commonly known as the 30-year shipbuilding plan. OPNAV N9I in coordination with the OPNAV ship resource and platform sponsor and COMNAVSEASYSCOM shall decide the lay-up and maintenance category assigned the ship (see paragraphs 6 and 7 for additional information).

3. <u>Projected Ship Inactivation Schedule Announcement</u>. CNO N9 shall release a naval administrative message no later than the fourth quarter of the FY, disseminating anticipated retirement dates for all vessels projected to retire in the upcoming FY.

4. <u>Submission of OPNAV 5400/1</u>. Per reference (h) and as discussed in chapter 2, COMUSFLTFORCOM and COMPACFLT must submit an OPNAV 5400/1 in support of the inactivation and retirement of all ships (except MSC ships) under the fleet's OPCON.

    a. For nuclear-powered ships, OPNAV 5400/1 provides a planned inactivation availability start date and a projected decommissioning date.

        (1) The start date for the inactivation process must be within the CNO approved inactivation FY.

        (2) For the final release of remaining crew members, the projected decommissioning date need not be in the same FY as the inactivation date. Except for aircraft carriers, this typically occurs 9 to 12 months after the inactivation start date.

    b. For non-nuclear-powered ships, OPNAV 5400/1 provides the retirement date for the ships. The retirement date must be within the CNO approved FY. This allows lead time for the ship's crew to complete their portion of the inactivation process.

    c. For changes in retirement date, COMUSFLTFORCOM and COMPACFLT are required to notify OPNAV N9I in the case of a change to a ship's retirement date or in the case of a nuclear-powered vessel retirement date, when the change does not cross FYs. In the event that a change is authorized that crosses FYs, a new OPNAV 5400/1 must be submitted per reference (h).

5. <u>Modernization</u>

    a. Alterations and improvements, if authorized, shall only be accomplished when vessels are undergoing full inactivation as identified in subparagraph 6b. In the case of FMS, the government-to-government agreement shall determine if alterations and improvements are to be accomplished. Ships destined for either disposal or logistic support asset will not have any alterations or improvements accomplished. During the period that a ship is in the inactive ship inventory, alterations and improvements will not normally be accomplished; however, an OPNAV ship resource and platform sponsor may elect to have an alteration or improvement installed on a retention asset. If so elected, the OPNAV ship resource and platform sponsor, in-service engineering agent or activity (ISEA) or inventory manager (IM) is responsible for funding the alteration.

b. Per reference (b), vessels shall not be modified or modernized within 5 years of retirement or disposal, except for safety alterations and modifications, certain other categories of modifications that fall within exceptions from this statute, or modifications for which a secretarial waiver is obtained. See the ASN (RD&A) Memo, "Guidance for Implementing Statute Prohibiting Modifications of a Weapons Platform within Five Years of Disposal," of 4 December 2012 for further guidance and procedures to comply with this statute.

c. Records of alterations, repairs, and other material changes for individual ships and service craft are essential to proper activation planning and will be kept up to date as directed by COMNAVSEASYSCOM. All configuration changes shall be reported using the OPNAV 4790/CK Ship's Configuration Change Form via the normal routing. Once records have reached the end of their life-cycle with COMNAVSEASYSCOM, they will be disposed of per SECNAV Manual 5210.1 of January 2012.

6. <u>Lay-up Categories</u>. Naval vessels are laid up for long-term storage or for safe storage pending disposal (see appendix D for a typical vessel's life cycle). The lay-up category determines the amount of maintenance and repair that should be performed prior to or during the inactivation. Lay-up category will be identified as part of the COMNAVSEASYSCOM ship inactivation plan. Maintenance procedures to meet these requirements shall be established by COMNAVSEASYSCOM. The categories are: standard inactivation, full inactivation, and safe stowage inactivation. Vessel lay-up categories will be assigned during the SDR.

a. <u>Standard Inactivation</u>. This type of inactivation is performed on vessels designated to be retained on the Naval Vessel Register as retention assets for possible future reactivation (OCIR or OSIR status). The ship and its equipment are to be preserved in an as-is condition to minimize long-term degradation and maintain the ship's condition at retirement. Ships designated for retention for longer than 4 years will receive a standard inactivation plan. All casualty reporting system, casualty categories of C-3 and C-4 casualty ratings per reference (j), require correction before retirement unless the responsible OPNAV ship resource and platform sponsor waives this requirement.

    b. <u>Full Inactivation</u>. A standard inactivation that includes pre-inactivation ship overhaul and dry docking.

    c. <u>Safe Stowage Inactivation</u>. This type of inactivation is performed on vessels that are to be stricken from the Naval Vessel Register and designated for disposal (to include foreign transfer and donation). Safe stowage inactivation is intended to accomplish the minimum work necessary to make the vessel safe for storage (e.g., fire and flooding protection) and to prevent environmental releases. The ship's material condition is expected to deteriorate if not disposed of in a timely manner, which may require emergent repairs or remediation to prevent an environmental regulatory violation.

7. <u>Maintenance Categories</u>

    a. Inactive ships and service craft are assigned to maintenance categories by COMNAVSEASYSCOM in coordination with OPNAV N9I based on the planned disposition. The categories indicate the priority sequence for the level of maintenance to be accomplished. The categories include maintenance categories B, C, D, I, X, and Z.

    b. Maintenance category definitions are as follows:

    (1) Maintenance category B is applicable to ships only. Category B ships are designated for potential mobilization and should receive the maximum maintenance, including improvement of material condition within funds available. Category B ships receive a standard or full inactivation lay-up.

    (2) Maintenance category C ships and service craft are those retention assets that will be maintained in an as-is material condition. The difference in category B and C is strictly in the prioritization of year-to-year maintenance

funds. Retention service craft will be assigned to category C per reference (a). Category C ships receive a standard inactivation lay-up.

(3) Maintenance category D ships and service craft are those in custody of the COMNAVSEASYSCOM INACTSHIPMAINTO sites, providing only berthing (not considered inactive but temporarily retained in an as-is condition on a reimbursable basis pending planned usage by the active force).

(4) Maintenance category I craft are in-service craft assigned to a COMNAVSEASYSCOM INACTSHIPMAINTO.

(5) Maintenance category X applies to ships and service craft that have been stricken from the Naval Vessel Register and are awaiting disposal by any method. Only security required for fire, flooding, and pilferage shall be provided, dehumidification and cathodic protection should not be maintained on inactive ships designated for FMS and donation hold unless authorized by OPNAV N9I.

(6) Maintenance category Z applies to former nuclear-powered ships and submarines plus nuclear-related tenders and service craft.

8. Split Inactivations. Split inactivations are situations where the inactivation process is begun in homeport and completed at a naval shipyard or other location before transferring the vessel to a COMNAVSEASYSCOM INACTSHIPMAINTO site. Split inactivations most commonly occur in the case of forward-deployed naval forces (FDNF) assigned ships or MSC ships assigned to the forward operating areas. In split inactivations, some of the following special provisions are made:

a. Equipage and consumables, which are required for crew comfort, propulsion plant operation, and ship control functions should be offloaded after arrival at the final inactivation site. Ships designated for FMS hold shall be required to follow chapter 6 and reference (i).

b. Change in status from active to in commission, in reserve, should take place upon arrival at the final inactivation site.

c. Changes in OPCON and ADCON responsibilities are as follows:

    (1) Fleet commander is responsible until arrival at a naval shipyard or inactive ship maintenance facility.

    (2) Upon arrival at a naval shipyard or inactive ship maintenance facility, COMNAVSEASYSCOM is responsible.

d. Budgeting and funding will be per chapter 9.

9. <u>Habitability</u>. During the inactivation availability phase, and at such time as the ship becomes uninhabitable for the remaining crew members, messing and berthing shall be provided. Arrangements and funding shall be the responsibility of the respective TYCOM; however, permanently installed berthing, messing facilities, laundry facilities, and habitability items should be held in a maximum state of readiness for reactivation consistent with proper preservation and security. Department of the Navy (DON), Office of the Assistant Secretary of the Navy, Financial Management and Comptroller Financial Management Policy Manual (NAVSO P-1000), section 075158, defines responsibility.

CHAPTER 4
THE SHIP DISPOSITION DECISION PROCESS

1. General

    a. SECNAV approves changes to the status of all naval
vessels, active or inactive (including MSC ships), and acts upon
the recommendations made by CNO. The ship disposition process
provides CNO with the following important pieces of information
for review: the proposed FY for a ship's retirement over the
FYDP, the proposed ship disposition, and the composition and
material condition of the current inactive ship inventory.

    b. The ship disposition process identifies which vessels
will inactivate, retire, or transfer from the fleet over the
FYDP. It also identifies which ships are to be transferred to
or retired from the active and NRF, and determines and validates
the disposition of those ships transferred to the inactive ship
maintenance facilities. This chapter addresses the procedures
required to manage the Navy's inactive inventory. Regardless of
a ship's disposition, a curator survey shall be performed within
12 months of the ship's retirement. See chapter 11 for
additional information on curator items.

    c. There are two critical events that take place to support
the overall ship disposition decision process. The first event
is the SID conference to determine the requirement for
inactivation and to identify the specific ships that will be
inactivated or decommissioned. The second event is the SDR
conference to determine the disposition of ships to be
inactivated and validate the disposition of the current inactive
ship inventory.

2. SID Conference

    a. The SID conference shall convene to determine which
vessels, including MSC vessels, to select for inactivation over
the FYDP in support of the upcoming budget cycle based on force
structure requirements, mission requirements, and budgetary
constraints. This meeting shall be chaired by OPNAV N9I.
Representatives shall include CNO N2/N6 and OPNAV (N42, N43,
N45, N84/ONR, N95, N96, N97, N98) ship resource and platform
sponsors, CNO N1 and CNO N4, Office of Budget/Fiscal Management
Division (FMB), INSURV, COMNAVSEASYSCOM, fleet commanders

(COMUSFLTFORCOM, COMPACFLT), TYCOMs (Commander, Naval Air
Forces, Atlantic (COMNAVAIRLANT); Commander, Naval Air Forces,
Pacific (COMNAVAIRPAC); Commander, Naval Surface Forces,
Atlantic (COMNAVSURFLANT); Commander, Naval Surface Forces,
Pacific (COMNAVSURFPAC); Commander, Submarine Forces
(COMSUBFOR); Commander, Submarine Forces, Pacific (COMSUBPAC),
and MSC), and USMC. Representatives are to be prepared to make
recommendations for CNO and SECNAV approval with regard to ship
inactivations and retirements, their financial impacts, and
other matters under their cognizance. The SID shall convene to
address the following:

(1) Identify vessels for inactivation that are
approaching their ESL during the FYDP.

(2) Identify ships whose ESLs need to be extended.

(3) Identify vessels that will not reach ESL during the
FYDP, giving consideration to design changes or modifications
that are determined as impracticable to a key operational system
upgrade, making it economically inappropriate to continue the
operation of that vessel.

(4) Describe any potential gaps in warfighting,
mobilization, or training capability that may occur as a result
of a vessel's inactivation.

(5) Consider the required material condition inspection
results and recommendations to determine a vessel's operational
effectiveness and interoperability.

b. Results of the SID will be disseminated as a baseline
for use in the next POM and the next report to congress on the
annual long-range plan for construction of naval vessels.

3. <u>SDR Conference</u>

a. The SDR will normally occur after the SID and shall be
chaired by OPNAV N9I and specifically address ships inactivating
in the current POM. Representatives shall include all OPNAV
ship resource and platform sponsors (CNO N2/N6 and OPNAV N42,
N43, N45, N84/ONR, N95, N96, N97, and N98), MARAD, OPNAV (N43,
N45, N52), Deputy Assistant Secretary of the Navy, Ships (DASN
(Ships)), FMB, INSURV, Navy IPO, COMNAVSEASYSCOM, fleet

commanders (COMUSFLTFORCOM, COMPACFLT), TYCOMs (COMNAVAIRLANT, COMNAVAIRPAC, COMNAVSURFLANT, COMNAVSURFPAC, COMSUBFOR, COMSUBPAC, and MSC), USMC, and the Office of Legislative Affairs. The SDR shall convene to define all inactivation and disposition requirements for each vessel that is scheduled for retirement during the FYDP and review the status of ships currently held in the inactive ship inventory.

b. Specifically, the conference shall address the following:

(1) Define all requirements regarding the method of lay-up, maintenance categories, transfers, and disposals.

(2) Provide projected inactivation or decommissioning and out-of-service dates within the FY addressed at the SID conference for all battle force and non-battle force ships.

(3) Identify requirements for inactive vessel utilization in fleet training exercises and experimental use during the FYDP.

c. The SDR results shall be reviewed and disseminated per congressional guidance. The FY 2008 Senate Armed Services Committee Report 110-77 required an appendix be added to the annual long-range plan for the construction of naval vessels that addresses the Navy's plan for decommissioning battle force ships during the FYDP. The Navy shall include the following information in this report:

(1) Hull numbers of ships that are to be disposed by dismantling or fleet training exercise within the FYDP.

(2) Hull numbers of battle force ships that are to be retired within the FYDP.

(3) Gaps in capability that will occur upon the retirement of each ship, including duration of that capability gap.

(4) Disposition proposed for each ship identified under subparagraph 3(c)(2) upon retirement.

4. <u>Disposition</u>. Appendix E graphically portrays some of the considerations used in determining the disposition of inactivating ships. Based on the results from the ship inactivation process, the following will be considered:

a. <u>Retention</u>. In support of meeting future U.S. Navy requirements, retain the vessel in the inactive ship inventory in an OCIR status or OSIR status. These vessels shall remain on the Naval Vessel Register while in a retention status.

b. <u>Non-Retention</u>. The vessel is processed for permanent removal from the Navy's inventory if the vessel is determined excess to the Navy's requirements or surplus. The vessel will be considered for use as a logistic support asset - primarily for the remaining ships in its class, fleet training exercise support (per reference (e)), experimental use, or evaluated for removal via one of the disposition methods listed in chapter 5.

CHAPTER 5
SHIP DISPOSITION POLICY

1. <u>General</u>. Select conventionally-powered ships that have completed their useful service lives may be retained in the inactive ship inventory for a period of time to be available for future mobilization or while awaiting disposal. The Navy's methods to reduce the inactive ship inventory include interagency transfers to the MARAD, U.S. Coast Guard (USCG), National Ocean and Atmospheric Administration (NOAA), or other U.S. Federal agencies; donations for memorial and museum use as static public displays; foreign military transfers; dismantling and recycling; fleet training exercises; experimental use, including weapons effectiveness testing; or transfers to U.S. States, territories, or other political subdivisions thereof for use as artificial reefs. Appendix E provides a quick look at the disposition process for combatants and noncombatants.

   a. Nuclear-powered ships and submarines are dismantled and recycled, which is typically accomplished at a naval shipyard.

   b. Tenders with nuclear support facilities shall be maintained in storage at the designated naval shipyard until the nuclear support facility is decontaminated. After the release of the nuclear support facilities and subsequent issuance of a free release letter by COMNAVSEASYSCOM Nuclear Propulsion Division (NAVSEA 08), custody of the vessel may be transferred to COMNAVSEASYSCOM INACTSHIPOFF.

   c. Service craft with nuclear support facilities shall be maintained in storage at the designated naval shipyard until the nuclear support facility is decontaminated. After the release of the nuclear support facility and subsequent issuance of a free release letter by NAVSEA 08, the custodian shall maintain custody of the craft pending disposal by COMNAVSEASYSCOM.

2. <u>Action</u>. In order for vessels that are transferred outside of Navy custody to no longer have the outward appearance of an active Navy vessel, names and numbers of naval vessels and service craft shall be painted out prior to transfer of custody outside the Navy, except for vessels donated for museum or memorial use.

3. <u>Disposal Methods</u>. The Navy's methods to reduce the inventory of inactive ships that have been stricken from the Naval Vessel Register include the following:

    a. <u>Interagency Transfer</u>. Requests for interagency transfers to MARAD, USCG, NOAA, or other U.S. Federal agencies are to be submitted to OPNAV N9I and are subject to SECNAV approval except as delegated by SECNAV to a lower level.

    (1) When Navy-owned ships stored in MARAD National Defense Reserve Fleet (NDRF) become excess, it is the Navy's policy that MARAD will, whenever possible, be given first disposition rights to the ship. MARAD transfers are authorized and governed by section 57101 of title 46, U.S.C., which provides that all Federal entities are authorized to transfer vessels to the NDRF without reimbursement subject to the approval of the Secretary of Transportation and the SECNAV with respect to Ready Reserve Force (RRF) vessels, and the Secretary of Transportation with respect to all other vessels, including Navy-owned ships not stored in MARAD's NDRF.

    (2) Transfers to other DoD agencies or the Department of Homeland Security are authorized and governed per section 2578 of reference (b).

    (3) Transfers to other U.S. Government Federal agencies outside of the DoD are authorized and governed by the Federal Property Act.

    b. <u>Intra-agency Transfer of Conventionally-powered Vessels</u>. Requests by a component of the DON for the transfer of a stricken naval vessel for conversion to an alternate use, non-destructive testing, or historic public display shall be submitted to OPNAV N9I for approval along with supporting justification for its use and demonstration of available budget authority to support its custody and proposed use. Transfers will be documented by a support agreement between COMNAVSEASYSCOM and the DON component agency per DoD Instruction 4000.19 of 25 April 2013. At the end of its proposed use, the DON component shall return the vessel to COMNAVSEASYSCOM custody per the intra-agency agreement. COMNAVSEASYSCOM shall be responsible for the disposal of such vessels after their return to COMNAVSEASYSCOM custody. For previous intra-agency transfers without intra-agency agreements in place consistent with this policy, COMNAVSEASYSCOM shall coordinate with the current custodian to establish plans for return of vessel custody to COMNAVSEASYSCOM and or ultimate disposal of the vessel.

c. <u>Ship Donation for Museum and Memorial Use</u>. Donated vessels serve as static public displays as museums and memorials that showcase and preserve naval history and tradition. Transfers to eligible Federal, State, and local governments and nonprofit organizations are to be at no cost to the United States per section 7306 of reference (b), except that vessels must be cosmetically demilitarized per DoD 4160.28-M, volume 1, Defense Demilitarization: Program Administration, of 7 June 2011. Ship donation is under the auspices of ASN (RD&A) and executed by COMNAVSEASYSCOM who will advise CNO of the final selection prior to public announcement. Transfers are subject to approval by the SECNAV. Only those vessels that are pending decommissioning and are determined to be historically significant or have a high probability of donation shall be considered. Re-designation of an inactive ship for donation from another disposal category is discouraged due to ship deterioration, equipment stripping, and or demilitarization or other disposal preparation work accomplished. Vessels shall not be typically retained in a donation hold status beyond 2 years unless authorized by ASN (RD&A) in consultation with OPNAV N9I. The designation of ships on donation hold may be extended on an annual basis at the SDR conference based on the existence of viable donation interest and demonstration by the prospective donee to COMNAVSEASYSCOM that measurable progress is being made toward submitting a donation application that meets the minimum COMNAVSEASYSCOM requirements. OPNAV N9I shall direct any change in the ship's disposition in consultation with ASN (RD&A). As donated vessels are transferred "as-is, where-is" any additional COMNAVSEASYSCOM responsibilities (whether custodial or financial) towards previously donated ships that require the use of funds provided under the operation and maintenance, Navy, 2B2G ship activations and inactivations budget line item and must be coordinated with the OPNAV resource sponsor for inactive ships, prior to assuming the responsibility, and include a detailed summary of expenditures utilized from the 2B2G budget line as part of the annual financial review with OPNAV N9I.

d. <u>FMS</u>. See chapter 6 for information regarding FMS.

e. Dismantling and Recycling (also known as "scrapping").
Pursuant to section 7305 and section 7305a of reference (b),
ship dismantling and recycling ensures the effective and
permanent demilitarization of a naval warship and prevents the
possibility of a ship in which U.S. military personnel have
served, fought, or died, from falling into undesirable hands or
being used for an objectionable purpose (e.g., commercial
display, property of an unfriendly government or group, or other
public indignity). Dismantling should be accomplished in the
United States or its territories whenever practicable per
existing laws and regulations. Excess weapons systems remaining
aboard will be demilitarized through complete destruction by the
ship dismantling contractor.

f. Artificial Reefing. Reference (c) provides guidance on
the preparation for reefing a ship. Pursuant to section 7306b
of reference (b), vessels stricken from the Naval Vessel
Register may be transferred by gift or otherwise to any State,
commonwealth, or possession of the United States or any
municipal corporation or political subdivision thereof for use
as artificial reefs. Transfers are subject to ASN (RD&A)
approval. COMNAVSEASYSCOM will notify the CNO of the final
selection prior to public announcement.

4. Environmental Preparation for Use in a Fleet Training
Exercise, Experimental Use, or Disposal.

a. Pursuant to section 7306a of reference (b), inactivated
non-nuclear ships may be used in fleet training exercise, or for
experimental use.

b. All ships shall be physically inspected to provide
reasonable assurance that no material of known or anticipated
value to the Navy remains aboard prior to disposal, use in a
fleet training exercise, or experimental use. The inspection
will be conducted by the COMNAVSEASYSCOM INACTSHIPOFF, or a
designated representative for non-nuclear ships, including ex-
Navy ships in the custody of MARAD. The inspector shall provide
written certification at the time of completion. The records
will be maintained at COMNAVSEASYSCOM INACTSHIPOFF for a period
of no less than 2 years after final disposal of the ship. Once
the records have reached the end of their life cycle with
COMNAVSEASYSCOM, the records shall be disposed of per SECNAV
Manual 5210.1 of January 2012.

5. <u>Vessels Supporting Fleet Training Exercises or Experimental Use</u>. Per reference (e), fleet and other major claimant requests for vessels in support of a fleet training exercise, target exercise, or experimental use must be submitted to COMNAVSEASYSCOM.

    a. Vessels used in training and experimental events are subject to environmental requirements as discussed in part 229 of title 40, Code of Federal Regulations, and per reference (c). These requirements include preparation of the vessel to minimize environmental impact, including removing fuel and other pollutants to the maximum extent practicable.

    b. The claimant shall submit a post sink exercise report by naval message per reference (c), identifying the location of the exercise including latitude, longitude, and water depth, to COMNAVSEASYSCOM WASHINGTON DC//SEA21// and CNO WASHINGTON DC//N001/N09/N4/N45/N43/N9/N9I//.

    c. At the end of the calendar year, COMNAVSEASYSCOM shall prepare an annual report for submission by OPNAV N45 to the EPA administrator per references (c) and (e).

CHAPTER 6
FOREIGN MILITARY TRANSFERS AND EXCESS DEFENSE ARTICLE SHIPS

1. General. Through FMS, the U.S. Navy is enhancing its own operational capabilities by ensuring the Navy's maritime partners are provided capable platforms. When considering vessels for FMS, the primary emphasis will be on accomplishing a hot ship transfer, which does not require inactivation and reactivation of a ship. Ship transfers that require inactivation and subsequent reactivation are discouraged unless a significant probability of transfer exists. Appendix C identifies the timeline for conducting critical actions in support of a ship being made available for foreign transfer.

2. Policy. Pursuant to section 7307 reference (b), a U.S. naval vessel that is in excess of 3,000 tons or that is less than 20 years of age may not be disposed of to another nation (whether by sale, lease, grant, loan, barter, transfer, or otherwise) unless the disposal of that vessel is authorized by law. Reference (i) is the governing Navy policy for the transfer of naval vessels to foreign governments, to include the ship's preparation for transfer and equipment disposition. Transfers are to be conducted at no cost to the U.S. Government with the exception of the removal of installed equipment that is non-transferable technology. Reference (i) does not apply to the delivery of new ships constructed under Navy contract for foreign governments. FMS vessels shall be stricken from the Naval Vessel Register prior to custody transfer to a foreign government.

3. Ship Disposition Process. Recommendations for designating specific vessels for foreign transfer shall be formalized as part of the CNO's SDR process (see chapter 4). During the SDR, OPNAV N52, in coordination with the Navy IPO, identifies specific vessels that the Navy's maritime partners (or the CNO) recommend be made available for foreign military transfer. The SDR reviews whether a ship will be transferred in a hot or cold status. Ships identified for FMS are reviewed annually as part of the SDR process to ensure valid requirements exist and that transfer legislation exists or is being sought. OPNAV N9I will determine the lay-up and maintenance category to be assigned to these ships while in the inactive inventory.

4. FMS

    a. Hot Ship Transfers. Per reference (i), a hot ship transfer occurs when the foreign crew "relieves the watch" of the U.S. Navy crew coincident with the decommissioning (or out-of-service date) of the ship from the U.S. Navy. In order for an inactivating ship to undergo a successful hot ship transfer, ship transfer legislation must be enacted no later than 18 months prior to the scheduled decommissioning or out-of-service date. Otherwise, the ship is directed to prepare for a safe stowage inactivation and lay-up in the inactive inventory in support of a future cold transfer unless directed otherwise by OPNAV N9I.

    b. Cold Ship Transfers. Ships designated for FMS that do not have transfer legislative authority in place 18 months prior to the scheduled retirement date are directed to undergo inactivation availability. COMNAVSEASYSCOM will provide the ship with an inactivation plan based on the ship's disposition no later than 180 days prior to the scheduled retirement date. During the inactivation availability – which typically starts 90 days ahead of the ship's retirement date - the TYCOM shall maintain oversight over the removal of equipment discussed in paragraph 7 and reference (i). If no viable transfer or candidate is identified within 2 years of inactivation, OPNAV N9I may redesignate the vessel for disposal in a manner most advantageous to the government.

5. Inspections by INSURV and Material Condition Assessments. The intent is to conduct a material condition assessment as early as possible in the transfer process to prepare a more accurate letter of offer and acceptance (LOA); reduce risk of work creep during reactivation and refurbishment; and reduce the risk from the ship transfer timeline. COMNAVSEASYSCOM is responsible for budgeting FMS administrative funding for material condition assessments of ships proposed for cold transfer. As part of the annual FMS administrative POM and budgeting processes, COMNAVSEASYSCOM shall submit requirements within the excess defense articles program element to Navy IPO. No funding from the 2B2G operations and maintenance, Navy budget line shall be used in support of material condition assessments.

    a. Hot Ship Transfers. Surveys will need to be conducted no later than 18 months prior to transfer - assuming congressional authorization for the transfer is in place. A survey is not required if the last material inspection or TYCOM mid-cycle assessment occurred within 3 years of the ship's retirement date.

b. Cold Ship Transfers. Post-inactivation material condition assessment will be scheduled if required by COMNAVSEASYSCOM and Navy IPO. If feasible, COMNAVSEASYSCOM may coordinate with Navy IPO to use FMS administrative funding for personnel to observe the last INSURV material inspection prior to the ship's inactivation.

6. Funding Associated with the Permanent Removal of Ships from the Navy's Inactive Ship Inventory.

a. Hot Ship Transfer. FMS case funding starts when the LOA has been accepted and countersigned. In the course of executing a "hot ship" transfer, all costs related to the transfer of the naval vessel that the U.S. Navy would not otherwise incur when inactivating or decommissioning the vessel must be borne by the recipient. Costs may include ship support for on-the-job training, additional fuel costs, supplies, messing, berthing, and equipment repairs attributed to system operation specifically in support of the hot ship transfer.

b. Cold Ship Transfer. FMS funding starts when the LOA has been accepted and countersigned. All charges are to accrue to the applicable FMS case except for the removal of non-transferable technology equipment, the cost of which will be borne by the OPNAV resource and platform sponsor or the equipment IM.

7. Equipment Removal from FMS. It is Navy policy that support of the active fleet remains a priority in dealing with equipment and material recovery in ship disposition issues. However, in the case of vessels designated for FMS, retiring ships shall not be stripped of equipment. Stripping of ships provides diminished operational capability to the Navy's maritime partners and erodes Navy's efforts to build maritime partner capacity. Guidance for the removal and retention of equipment and supplies for ships designated for FMS can be found per reference (i). Installed equipment (e.g., combat; command, control, communications, computers, and intelligence (C4I); and hull, mechanical, and electrical systems) shall not be stripped

from inactivating ships unless specifically authorized by OPNAV N9I per subparagraph 7b. Emergent logistic requirements will always be considered on a case-by-case basis to support the fleet.

a. In support of the fleet releasing its "decommissioning" guidance to respective ships, COMNAVSEASYSCOM, in coordination with Navy IPO, shall issue a naval message to the TYCOM not later than 7 months prior to retirement, copy OPNAV N9I, respective OPNAV ship resource and platform sponsor, and COMNAVSEASYSCOM program sponsor identifying non-transferable technology (to include combat systems) required to be removed from the vessel. COMNAVSEASYSCOM, in coordination with the Commander, Space and Naval Warfare Systems Command (COMSPAWARSYSCOM) or Commander, Naval Air Systems Command (COMNAVAIRSYSCOM) as appropriate, will also address the viability of sanitizing on-board classified systems to an acceptable level if the equipment is designated to be retained aboard and transferred with the vessel.

b. No additional installed equipment removals shall be permitted except as specifically authorized by OPNAV N9I in response to a record request submitted by Program Executive Office for Integrated Warfare Systems or respective COMNAVSEASYSCOM ship program offices not later than 9 months prior to the ship's retirement date except in the case of emergent casualties in the casualty reporting system, casualty categories of C-3 and C-4 casualty ratings per reference (j), that includes:

(1) A comprehensive list (by individual ship) of specific installed equipment desired for removal.

(2) Justification for the removal.

(a) Evidence that the Navy supply system is unable to fulfill the requirement.

(b) TYCOM and regional maintenance center is unable to fulfill the requirement.

(3) An assessment of the ability to restore the equipment in operational condition in the event the vessel transfers as a cold FMS ship, and includes coordination via the respective systems command (SYSCOM):

(a) COMSPAWARSYSCOM.

(b) COMNAVSEASYSCOM.

(c) COMNAVAIRSYSCOM.

(d) COMNAVSUPSYSCOM.

c. Classified equipment shall be removed, sanitized, or declassified by the ship's custodian per instructions from the cognizant SYSCOM or IM. Technical assistance or labor required for such action shall be furnished by the cognizant SYSCOM or IM at the request of the custodian.

d. Reference (i) provides the list of equipment that must be removed prior to FMS transfer.

e. Preferred historical items, as desired by the curator of the Navy, will be forwarded per chapter 11.

f. For any questions regarding transferability of equipment to foreign nations not addressed per reference (i), direct liaison is authorized between TYCOM and Navy IPO in conjunction with the appropriate SYSCOM and info to OPNAV N9I.

g. Appendix B provides general guidance on equipment removals during the inactivation availability, however, reference (i) is the governing instruction for equipment in support of all FMS transfers.

8. Final Disposition. OPNAV N52 in coordination with Navy IPO shall provide OPNAV N9I and the custodian for the Naval Vessel Register copies of the vessel delivery certificates.

9. Modernization. In the case of FMS, the government-to-government agreement will determine if alterations and improvements are to be accomplished.

CHAPTER 7
STRIKING POLICY

1. <u>General</u>. It is Navy's policy that all naval vessels listed in the Naval Vessel Register be stricken prior to being permanently removed from U.S. Navy's custody as provided for in section 7304 through section 7308 of reference (b), which includes vessels removed in support of a fleet training exercise, experimental use, interagency transfer, FMS, artificial reefing, donation as a museum or memorial, and dismantlement. Vessels being retained in support of future mobilization purposes shall not be stricken from the Naval Vessel Register until declared excess to DON requirements.

2. <u>Authority</u>. Upon recommendations made by CNO, SECNAV authorizes the striking of ships from the Naval Vessel Register. DASN (Ships) has the authority to approve the striking of support and service craft (excluding submersibles) from the Naval Vessel Register. Specific direction is given to COMNAVSEASYSCOM to develop and execute the process for striking service craft from the Naval Vessel Register per reference (a).

a. <u>Non-Nuclear Ships</u>. Whenever practicable, non-nuclear ships will be stricken from the Naval Vessel Register effective the date of their retirement unless held as a retention asset.

b. <u>Nuclear-Powered Vessels</u>. Nuclear-powered ships shall be stricken from the Naval Vessel Register concurrent with the date of their decommissioning. Nuclear-powered vessels shall be placed in an in commission, in reserve status as of the date of the start of their inactivation availability and decommissioned upon release of the crew following fuel removal.

3. <u>Action</u>. During the fourth quarter of the FY, CNO N9 shall submit an action memorandum to SECNAV, via CNO, recommending specific ships and submarines scheduled to inactivate or retire during the forthcoming FY (other than those designated for retention) be stricken from the Naval Vessel Register, commensurate with their date of retirement. This action memorandum shall also include a disposal recommendation for conventional vessels. Specifically, the action memorandum shall include the following:

a. Identify each vessel recommended for striking and include its ESL, current age, proposed date of inactivation or retirement, and planned disposition.

b. Certify combatant vessels contained in the memorandum are not essential to the defense of the United States per section 7308 of reference (b).

4. Records. For accounting and recording purposes, a copy of the strike action memorandum will be provided to the Naval Vessel Register custodian to affect updates to the Naval Vessel Register database and Web site.

CHAPTER 8
REACTIVATION

1. Mobilization

a. Reactivation of inactive ships and service craft under conditions of total, full, or partial mobilization will be governed by the general instructions contained in the current operation plans (OPLAN) and such other mobilization plans as may be issued by the CNO.

b. When tasked by the OPNAV ship resource and platform sponsor, COMNAVSEASYSCOM is responsible for the preparation of plans and programs for the reactivation, repair, modernization, and fitting out of inactive ships and service craft in support of mobilization plans. COMNAVSEASYSCOM is also responsible for the planning for reactivation, initial procurement of material, managing funds, and allocating the industrial resources required for mobilization. Outfitting and trials shall be accomplished per OPNAVINST 4700.8J.

c. Mobilization plans of military personnel for the ordering of crews to ships being activated will be provided per the OPLANs.

d. Fleet commanders will plan for and execute training of the crews upon mobilization and will accept custody of the ships when reactivation has been completed and the ship is returned to active status.

e. Mobilization plans for the timely issue of communications security publications and equipment to ships and service crafts upon reactivation will be provided by CNO N2/N6 as required.

f. Mobilization plans for the fitting out of reactivated ships and service craft with ECDIS-N or navigational charts and publications shall be provided by the Oceanographer of the Navy (OPNAV N2/N6E).

2. Other than Mobilization. Reactivation, repair, modernization, and fitting out of ships and service craft under circumstances other than mobilization shall be under cognizant direction issued by the CNO.

CHAPTER 9
PLANNING, PROGRAMMING, BUDGETING, AND EXECUTION

1. General. OPNAV N9I assesses and manages the requirements generation process for all OPNAV resource and platform sponsors to facilitate the programming of funding for inactivation, maintenance, and disposal of naval ships under the ship activation and inactivation 2B2G budget line. COMNAVSEASYSCOM is responsible for execution of funding from these lines.

2. Non-Nuclear-Powered Ship Programming and Budgeting. Requirements to be included are: facilities costs for each COMNAVSEASYSCOM INACTSHIPMAINTO plus COMNAVSEASYSCOM INACTSHIPOFF, overhead costs, total amount required for inactivation that includes any effort to be undertaken by the TYCOM to effect inactivation work, costs to maintain the inactive ship inventory and infrastructure, ship disposal costs, and personnel costs.

    a. Under all circumstances, respective OPNAV ship resource and platform sponsors and, where applicable, MSC are responsible for funding the ship's inactivation lay-up and first year's maintenance in the inactive ship inventory.

    b. OPNAV N9I is responsible for the cost of the second and subsequent years' maintenance in the inactive ship inventory and for ship disposal costs.

    c. For submarine tenders, OPNAV N97 is responsible for the cost of the second and subsequent years' maintenance in shipyard storage and funding nuclear support facility decontamination. Following decontamination and release, OPNAV N9I is responsible for the maintenance and ship disposal costs.

    d. OPNAV ship resource and platform sponsors electing to perform alterations or improvements on inactive ships will fund the effort out of the appropriate resource sponsor's budget line.

    e. Funding for ashore berthing and messing of crew required for the inactivation process will be the responsibility of the respective TYCOM.

f. Donated vessels are transferred "as-is, where-is."
COMNAVSEASYSCOM is not authorized to use funds provided under
2B2G budget line towards previously donated ships without the
concurrence of the OPNAV resource sponsor for inactive ships.
COMNAVSEASYSCOM will include as part of the annual financial
review with the OPNAV resource sponsor a detailed summary of
funds expended from the 2B2G budget line to support previously
donated vessels.

3. <u>Nuclear-Powered Ship Programming and Budgeting</u>.
Requirements to be included are: advanced planning, ship
inactivation, reactor compartment disposal, decontamination, and
hull recycling. The OPNAV ship resource and platform sponsor is
responsible for programming and budgeting the activities listed
above. If, following defueling and inactivation and prior to
disposal, the hull for a nuclear-powered ship is placed in
storage, programming and budgeting for storage shall be as
follows:

    a. The OPNAV ship resource and platform sponsor (OPNAV N96,
N97, and N98) is responsible for funding the ship's inactivation
layup and first year's maintenance in storage.

    b. The OPNAV ship resource and platform sponsor (OPNAV N96,
N97, and N98) is responsible for the cost of storage of defueled
nuclear-powered ships. Resource sponsor is responsible for the
storage in the inactive inventory while awaiting final
disposition.

    c. Funding for ashore berthing and messing of crew required
for the inactivation process shall be the responsibility of the
respective TYCOM.

4. <u>Funding for Placing a USNS Out of Service</u>. Costs associated
with the pre-inactivation effort, initial inactivation, and
first year's lay-up in the inactive fleet for MSC ships are the
execution year responsibility of MSC. The OPNAV ship resource
and platform sponsor, via the cognizant customer budget
submitting office (BSO), is responsible for programming the
costs to both retiring the vessel as well as the costs
associated with the vessel's first year's lay-up in the inactive
fleet. Such costs shall be programmed as reimbursable funding
for use by MSC in the appropriation and budget line item under
which the ship's operations were funded while active. When

inactivation decisions are made outside the timeline supported by the programming process (e.g., an emergent inactivation), then it is the responsibility of the customer BSO to identify funds to support the above costs. Further costs associated with subsequent years' retention and disposal will be funded by OPNAV N9I.

5. <u>Other Costs</u>. OPNAV N9I is additionally responsible for programming the following costs:

    a. All military construction costs associated with maintaining the COMNAVSEASYSCOM INACTSHIPMAINTO, relocating a COMNAVSEASYSCOM INACTSHIPMAINTO, or maintaining shipyard assets to support hull storage.

    b. All military and civilian personnel at the COMNAVSEASYSCOM INACTSHIPOFF and the COMNAVSEASYSCOM INACTSHIPMAINTO.

6. <u>Funding Associated with Equipment Removals</u>. Costs for equipment removal, dismantling, packing, handling, and crating incidental to the delivery of stripped material intended for further use will be financed by the SYSCOM, other Service, or other authority directing removal and redistribution of subject material. In none of these situations will costs be incurred by COMNAVSEASYSCOM unless approved prior to equipment removal. Official notification to do such work is provided by the directing authority, accompanied by appropriate funding authorization. See chapter 12 for further explanation of the equipment removal policy. Specifically, certain common situations shall be handled as follows:

    a. Removal and shipment of equipment removed from retention assets by COMNAVSEASYSCOM INACTSHIPOFF in support of potential reactivation of the ship will normally be funded by the OPNAV ship resource and platform sponsor and executed by COMNAVSEASYSCOM out of the 2B2G budget line when commensurate with ship inactivation.

    b. Removal and shipment of equipment removed from retention or certain disposal assets for reutilization by IM will be funded out of the IM restoration funds.

c. Removal and shipment of equipment removed from retention or certain disposal assets for support of an immediate IM requirement (cannibalization) will be funded out of the IM's restoration funds. Replacement may be required and is the responsibility of the requesting activity.

d. Removal and shipment of equipment removed from disposal assets in support of TYCOM stripping during inactivation shall be funded by fleet maintenance funds.

e. Any costs associated with removing equipment from a ship prior to authorizing the ship for a fleet training exercise, experimental use or any other ship disposition method must be borne by the requesting fleet or BSO.

f. Removal, sanitization and shipment of equipment which must be removed or sanitized incidental to the hot transfer of a ship to a foreign government shall be financed by the group dictating removal.

7. Funds Associated with Preparation of Vessels Held for Experimental Purposes

a. Fleet commands are responsible for all environmental preparation costs for fleet training exercises, per reference (e). When practical, the requesting authority should check with fleet schedulers to determine if MSC assets are available to tow the vessel rather than contracting for commercial tow services.

b. For other than fleet training exercises, the requesting authority is responsible for environmental, storage and breakout preparation for ships held as targets or for experimental purposes.

c. The cost for towing shall be borne by the requesting authority.

8. Funding Associated with the Permanent Removal of Ships from the Navy's Inactive Ship Inventory

a. Ships Held for FMS. Transfers are to be conducted at no cost to the U.S. Government, except for removal of non-transferable equipment and the unmooring and release of the vessel to the receiving agent. In the case of a hot ship transfer, FMS case funding starts when the LOA has been accepted and countersigned. For a cold ship transfer, FMS funding starts when the FMS case is implemented. Chapter 6 is germane.

    b. <u>Ships Held for Donation or Transfer to Another Government Agency</u>. Transfers of ships that will be donated as a museum or memorial or transferred to another government agency are to be conducted at no cost to the Navy, except for the removal of non-transferable equipment and the unmooring and release of the vessel to the receiving agent. Any exceptions will be coordinated through the OPNAV ship resource and platform sponsor.

9. <u>Ships Held as Retention Assets</u>. OPNAV N9I shall program for the disposal of all non-nuclear assets that are removed from a retention status in the 2B2G budget line.

10. <u>Split Inactivations</u>. Split inactivations are situations where the inactivation process is begun in homeport and completed at a naval shipyard or other location before transferring the vessel to a COMNAVSEASYSCOM INACTSHIPMAINTO site. Split inactivations most commonly occur in the case of FDNF assigned to the forward operating areas. In split inactivations, funding responsibilities are as follows:

    a. Prior to the start of the inactivation, the TYCOM and COMNAVSEASYSCOM are responsible to share funding. Typically, normal crew type functions will be funded by TYCOM and other work will be centrally funded by COMNAVSEASYSCOM.

    b. At the start of inactivation at homeport, TYCOM and COMNAVSEASYSCOM are responsible to share funding. Typically, normal crew type functions will be funded by TYCOM and other work will be centrally funded by COMNAVSEASYSCOM.

    c. Upon arrival at the final inactivation site, COMNAVSEASYSCOM INACTSHIPMAINTO is responsible.

    d. Exceptions to the above funding responsibilities are as follows:

(1) For conventionally-powered ships, necessary removal and packing of equipage left aboard for the voyage to the COMNAVSEASYSCOM INACTSHIPMAINTO site will be at the expense of the TYCOM.

(2) Industrial assistance required to remove installed aviation support equipment shall be funded by either the TYCOM or the appropriate IM.

11. Action. COMNAVSEASYSCOM will provide OPNAV N9I with funding profiles and execution status reports for non-nuclear and nuclear-powered vessels as requested.

CHAPTER 10
INSPECTIONS AND MATERIAL READINESS POLICY

1. <u>General</u>. The objective of an inactivation material survey is to document the material condition of a ship designated for retention for future mobilization prior to inactivating. This is accomplished through the attainment and maintenance of effective preservation and the prevention of deterioration. A secondary objective is the accomplishment of repairs and improvements when they can be accomplished within the capability and availability of personnel and funds.

2. <u>Inspections by INSURV</u>

    a. Documentation of the material condition of each inactive ship is the end product of an inspection program.

    b. Policy contained in this instruction will take precedence, per references (f) and (g), when a ship is within 12 months of inactivating, with the following modification: regardless of a ship's disposal status, ships exceeding periodicity requirements, per references (f) and (g), will not conduct any portion of an overseas deployment or significant out-of-area operations without approval from OPNAV (N09P).

    (1) <u>OCIR and OSIR</u>. INSURV will conduct a survey on ships scheduled to inactivate and be retained in an OCIR or OSIR status within 18 months prior to the planned retirement date unless waived by OPNAV N9I. A material inspection conducted by INSURV within the 18-month period preceding inactivation shall fulfill the requirement of the survey.

    (2) <u>FMS Transfers</u>. Refer to chapter 6 for inspection requirements for ships designed for FMS transfer.

    (3) <u>Non-FMS Transfers</u>. Ships designated for reassignment to MSC, USCG, or other DoD or Federal agencies will receive a material inspection within 18 months of inactivating unless waived by OPNAV N9I.

    (4) <u>Sink Exercise or Disposal</u>. Ships designated for use for fleet training exercises, experimental use, or disposal shall not require a survey and should not be scheduled for a material inspection within 18 months of inactivation.

(5) <u>Inactive OCIR and OSIR Assets</u>. Surveys of inactive ships under the responsibility of COMNAVSEASYSCOM are performed on an as-needed basis.

c. The requirement for service craft inspections is specified per reference (a).

CHAPTER 11
CURATOR ITEMS REMOVAL POLICY

1. General

a. The curator for the DON is responsible for collection, preservation, and exhibition of naval relics, trophies, paintings, historical prints, photographs, and other naval memorabilia of historical significance. Presentation silver is the responsibility of COMNAVSUPSYSCOM and questions concerning its disposition shall be addressed to COMNAVSUPSYSCOM.

b. This chapter lists objects and items that will be removed from naval vessels on behalf of the curator in each category. The curator shall be informed of any other material of potentially historic significance that may come to the attention of ship custodians. Questions concerning the significance of any item shall be referred to the curator for resolution.

c. Regardless of a ship's disposal, a curator survey will be performed on all inactivating and retiring vessels within 12 months prior to decommissioning. Items identified by the curator during the curator survey must be removed prior to final disposal.

2. Curator Criteria. Generally, the criteria for evaluating curator interests are:

a. Association With

(1) Combat.

(2) Notable achievements.

(3) Memorable events.

(4) Mission roles and functions.

b. Unique or Special Significance From a Technical Viewpoint

c. Special Relationship with Personnel and Individuals

(1) Heroism.

(2) Humane efforts.

(3) Human interest.

(4) Vessel's sponsor.

3. Relics to be Removed and Forwarded to the Curator from Ships Being Decommissioned. The following is to be used as guidance and is not necessarily absolute. The definition of memorabilia can be subjective; therefore, vessel custodians are encouraged to use good judgment considering the historic nature of an object.

a. Bells. Ship's main bell and quarterdeck bell will be forwarded to the Navy curator. Foreign transfer end users are responsible for replacement of the bells prior to transfer.

b. Plaques

(1) Commissioning and builder plaques.

(2) CO plaques.

(3) Individually designed insignia plaque (and mold for same).

(4) Historical data plaques.

(5) Navy efficiency award plaques.

c. Distinctive Heraldic Materials

(1) Shoulder sleeve insignia.

(2) Unit identification marks.

d. Flags

(1) Final flags flown (national ensign, jack, commissioning pennant) shall be forwarded to the Navy curator.

(2) Flags flown in significant operations or in battle shall be forwarded to the Navy curator.

e. Loaned or Donated Property

(1) Sponsor gifts and loans must be reported to the curator for further disposition.

(2) Loaned items from a private person, public agency, or organization (silver service items excepted) shall be returned to their owners with a copy of the return documentation to the Navy curator.

f. Paintings and Photographs. Paintings and photographs of a naval nature shall be forwarded to the Navy curator.

g. Documents. Documents related to the history of the activity or command, to include citations, historical correspondence, commemorative brochures of special events and occasions, copies of command histories, briefing packets, command newspapers, technical books and manuals related to its operational mission. Typical items include:

(1) Commissioning brochure.

(2) Change of command brochure.

(3) Welcome aboard packet.

(4) Decommissioning brochure.

(5) Ships characteristic cards.

(6) Booklet of general plans.

(7) Campaign ribbons.

(8) Display boards

(a) One ship's name board.

(b) Special displays created on the vessel's history and heritage.

(9) Silver service. Shall be forwarded by ship's force to COMNAVSUPSYSCOM for disposition per Naval Supply Systems Command (NAVSUPSYSCOM).

(10) Trophies.

(11) Mission (specific material). Significant items for retention will be coordinated with the Navy curator, TYCOM, and material managers.

4. <u>Relics Which the Curator May Request from All Vessels Prior to Use in a Fleet Training Exercise or Disposal by Scrap, Experimental Use, or Title Transfer to MARAD</u>. The following is to be used as guidance and is not necessarily absolute. The definition of memorabilia can be subjective; therefore, vessel custodians are encouraged to use good judgment considering the historic nature of an object.

a. Anchors and anchor chain.

b. Anemometer.

c. Barometer.

d. Bells.

e. Clocks.

f. Communication material.

g. Engine order telegraph.

h. Engine room equipment.

i. Furniture.

j. Guns and guided missile launching systems.

k. Inclinometer and indicators.

l. Life ring buoys.

m. Mission specific material.

n. Navigational equipment.

o. Planking.

p. Plotting boards.

q. Ship specific equipment.

r. Signaling equipment.

s. Steering stand.

t. Submarine specific equipment.

u. Gun tompions.

v. Wheels.

w. Electronic warfare material.

5. <u>Address Where Curator Items Shall Be Forwarded</u>

SHIP TO:
Curator for the Department of the Navy
Naval History and Heritage Command
Building 46
Washington Navy Yard
805 Kidder Breese Street SE
Washington, DC 20374-5060
(202) 433-2842/5858

CHAPTER 12
EQUIPMENT REMOVAL POLICY

1. General

a. Appendix B contains listings of material and items to be off-loaded according to the disposition of the ship. Even these listings, prepared with the assistance of interested SYSCOMs, bureaus, and offices must be regarded as guides and not absolute. Authority to deviate from this list is determined by OPNAV N9I.

b. Once a ship has been turned over to COMNAVSEASYSCOM INACTSHIPOFF, or a nuclear-powered vessel has been turned over to a naval shipyard, the equipment, controlled equipage, and repair parts that are authorized for removal shall be replaced in the case of reactivation, unless the vessel is designated for disposal, or unless replacement is waived by OPNAV N9I and recorded in the ship's inactivation plan.

2. Cannibalizations. Removal shall be conducted per reference (k). Removal requests will be supported to the maximum extent possible from non-retention assets and will support casualty report (CASREP) requirements only. NAVSUPSYSCOM Weapon Systems Support manages cannibalization requests.

a. Paybacks are required within 12 months for components removed from retention assets unless waived by OPNAV N9I. Paybacks are not required for vessels designated as a non-retention asset.

b. For donation hold assets, cannibalization without replacement is authorized provided equipment removal does not disturb the cosmetic appearance of the ship, in which case a cosmetic carcass may be substituted in lieu of a payback in kind. COMNAVSEASYSCOM is the approval authority for these actions.

3. Equipment Removal

a. Per reference (i), ships designated for transfer to a foreign government must not be stripped except as specifically authorized by OPNAV N9I, in coordination with COMNAVSEASYSCOM and Navy IPO. See chapter 6 and reference (i) for additional guidance on equipment removals from ships designated as potential FMS assets.

b. The priority for ship equipment removals shall be established by COMNAVSEASYSCOM; however, TYCOM shall have priority when there is an immediate cannibalization request from COMUSFLTFORCOM or COMPACFLT. In addition to storeroom and operating space items, each system and equipment life cycle IM, in consultation with appropriate COMNAVSEASYSCOM code, will carefully screen all installed assets for insurance items and prioritize the items that have the highest risk and longest lead time for repair. The COMNAVSEASYSCOM INACTSHIPMAINTO, in coordination with OPNAV ship resource and platform sponsors, will take actions to have identified items from the prioritized list removed and refurbished and certified as ready for issue and then placed in proper storage for potential use.

c. Equipment removed during a ship's inactivation availability shall be authorized by TYCOM in coordination with COMNAVSEASYSCOM and the ISEA or IM.

d. During inactive ship storage with COMNAVSEASYSCOM, all equipment removals are managed by COMNAVSEASYSCOM. Paybacks are required within 12 months for components removed from retention and foreign transfer designated assets unless waived by OPNAV N9I. Paybacks are not required for vessels designated as a non-retention asset. Equipment removals should be coordinated with the OPNAV ship resource and platform sponsor.

e. During disposal preparation, all equipment not affecting safe storage or personnel safety is available for removal. All equipment removals are managed by COMNAVSEASYSCOM INACTSHIPMAINTO Equipment Removal System (ERS). Activities removing installed equipment shall execute all planning in ERS. Once the items are removed, the requesting activity shall provide the COMNAVSEASYSCOM INACTSHIPMAINTO with the national item identification number, quantity requested, location, and point of contact details in the event the removed items are needed to support a future requirement (e.g., diminished manufacturing sources and material shortage case).

4. <u>Priority for Stripped Ship Material</u>. With the exception of ships designated for FMS transfer, the following priorities for material stripped from ships will be observed:

a. The curator of the Navy shall have first priority to remove designated items of historical interest. Such items will normally be removed during the inactivation availability.

b. IMs have first priority on the removal of installed equipment, controlled equipage, and repair parts (including storeroom items, maintenance assist modules (MAM), and ready service spares) for which a known or anticipated requirement exists.

c. TYCOM shall direct redistribution of all general use consumables and non-controlled equipage to other fleet units. Installed equipment, controlled equipage, and repair parts not designated by IM for turn-in prior to decommissioning may be redistributed by the fleet commanders for immediate use or to fill allowance deficiencies.

d. COMNAVSEASYSCOM INACTSHIPMAINTO has priority, after active fleet and NRF ship requirements are met, to remove materials or equipment to fill allowance deficiencies in selected reserve maintenance category B ships.

e. The fleet commanders (COMUSFLTFORCOM and COMPACFLT), using their CNO designation as area coordinators, may authorize naval activities within their geographical area to remove material or equipment. After higher priority requirements have been met, fleet commanders may issue material in the following order of priority:

(1) Naval activities.

(2) Naval Reserve and Fleet Reserve activities.

(3) USCG activities and other government agencies.

f. Prior to ship disposal and after all other equipment stripping requirements are satisfied, stricken ships at COMNAVSEASYSCOM INACTSHIPMAINTO facilities may be open to existing naval ship museum organizations to support the restoration of existing museum ships. Material donation transfers are to be documented with a DD Form 1149 Requisition and Invoice/Shipping Document.

g. COMNAVSEASYSCOM will approve any extensions in ship disposal schedules necessary for the removal of equipment and material necessary to support the active fleet.

5. Stripping Procedures

a. Stripping and the transfer of custody of decommissioned and stricken ships will use the following guidelines:

(1) Stripping in advance of the ship's retirement or strike date shall commence only when specifically authorized by the TYCOM. Modifications and limitations to the general stripping policy included in this instruction will be specified in the disposal authorization, if required, dependent upon type of disposal selected.

(2) The CO of an active ship will perform the duties of a stripping activity (non-industrial) prior to retirement when advance stripping has been authorized.

(3) COMUSFLTFORCOM, COMPACFLT, or COMNAVSEASYSCOM, when requested by the CNO for ships which have not been delivered to a COMNAVSEASYSCOM INACTSHIPMAINTO, shall designate an appropriate custodian to take custody of the individual ship or service craft on, or subsequent to, the retirement date for active ships, or strike date for inactive ships. Such designated activities shall remain the custodian until the ship is delivered to a COMNAVSEASYSCOM INACTSHIPMAINTO.

b. All removal actions under inactivation will be subject to the following conditions:

(1) Coordination and control by the designated custodian (COMNAVSEASYSCOM INACTSHIPMAINTO, TYCOM, or other as appropriate).

(2) Removal of material will be accomplished with personnel or funds of the requesting activity except for active ships approved for disposal and authorized to conduct stripping in advance of retirement date.

c. When IMs are exercising their authority to remove material from active ships designated as candidates for strike, they will provide COMUSFLTFORCOM and COMPACFLT commanders, TYCOM, the appropriate COMNAVSEASYSCOM INACTSHIPMAINTO, or other designated stripping activities with lists of installed equipment, repair parts, and items of controlled equipage in critical shortage in the supply system. COMNAVSEASYSCOM is responsible for keeping all IMs advised of the intentions of the CNO to strike a ship from the Naval Vessel Register.

(1) When so advised, the IM shall forward a list of required equipment, obsolete items (current or planned), and repair parts to the activities concerned for use as a planning document.

(2) Fleet commanders will not initiate action on these lists until SECNAV approves and CNO announces the strike and authorizes advance stripping. Upon this announcement, material identified by the IM listings will be turned in to the supply system as expeditiously as resources permit.

(3) Allowable credit for material turned in by fleet personnel to satisfy the specific requirements of the IMs shall accrue to the fleet following normal credit procedures.

d. In exercising their redistribution rights, fleet commanders or TYCOMs will send an unclassified naval message to COMNAVSEASYSCOM, and copy to the CNO and the cognizant IM, providing information of the specific material(s) to be removed, and the specific ships to provide and receive the material prior to fleet redistribution of installed equipment. The IM will be allowed 10 days to reply if they desire to exercise their authority to reallocate this material. Fleet commanders or TYCOMs will establish a cut-off date during the period prior to the ship's decommissioning after which any requests received will be forwarded to the custodian or designated stripping activity.

e. Any installed equipment, which is not classified, not in critical supply and the removal of which is not economical, will be disposed of with the ship.

f.   Classified equipment will be removed or declassified by the custodian per instructions from the cognizant SYSCOM or IM. Technical assistance or labor required for such action will be furnished by the cognizant SYSCOM or IM at the request of the custodian.

g.   COMNAVSEASYSCOM will establish a deadline date for the completion of stripping (non-industrial) for each ship.

h.   OPNAV N9I will resolve, per procedures contained herein, all questions concerning priority requirements of material or equipment to be removed.

6.   <u>Reinstallation of Removed Equipment</u>.   All equipment removed from inactivating ships is subject to reinstallation if the disposition of the ship is retention asset or is designated for FMS.   The reinstallation of the equipment shall be funded and completed by the command responsible for the equipment removal.

CHAPTER 13
MILITARY SEALIFT COMMAND

1. <u>General</u>. This chapter sets forth the policy for activation and inactivation of ships to be assigned duty with MSC. Funding associated with MSC ships can be found in chapter 9, paragraph 4.

2. <u>Custody</u>. Custody of ships shall be transferred between COMNAVSEASYSCOM and MSC as mutually agreed. MSC ships designated for disposal upon inactivation will first be offered to the MARAD for title transfer upon arrival at a MARAD NDRF facility.

3. <u>Activation</u>

a. The responsibility, upon mobilization and under conditions other than mobilization, for the activation of ships assigned to the NDRF and held for MSC use rests with MSC. The ships will be activated, upon transfer of custody from MARAD to MSC, through a variety of ways selected by the MSC to fit the circumstances. MSC will be the contracting officer for the activation of ships for which MSC is responsible for the activation.

b. The cost of activation and repairs to ships activated in response to DoD requirements will be borne by MSC and recovered through billings to the customer BSO. Alterations, repairs, etc., that are military in character and directed to be accomplished by CNO, will be financed as directed by the CNO. Items requisitioned to fill deficiencies in equipment allowances and subsistence items shall be charged to the account for the ship.

c. Military equipment that is retained on board shall be maintained in a preserved status by MSC. When a ship is activated for MSC and is assigned to a fleet component within a period of 1 year after activation, the cost of activation shall be borne by the fleet component through billings from MSC.

d. For ships not controlled by MARAD, COMNAVSEASYSCOM shall provide MSC with disposition instructions for dehumidification equipment and portable gear removed. Dehumidification equipment installed by MARAD while ships are in the NDRF shall be removed and retained by MARAD during activation.

4. Return. Upon return of a ship to inactive status, the cost of the items required to fill deficiencies in the allowance list and to replenish the stock of consumable supplies shall be borne by MSC and recovered through billings to the customer BSO. The cost of overhaul prior to inactivation, when authorized, and the cost of inactivation of a ship returned directly to inactive status by MSC shall be borne by MSC and recovered through billings to the customer BSO. The cost of overhaul prior to inactivation, if required, and inactivation of a ship that was originally activated for MSC and subsequently transferred to a fleet unit, shall be borne by COMNAVSEASYSCOM under existing directives for the inactivation of ships assigned to the fleet.

5. Alterations. Alterations of a military character, directed by the CNO for accomplishment during activation, will be financed as directed by the CNO. Alterations of a non-military character that are accomplished during activation will be funded by MSC and billed to the appropriate BSO.

6. Disposition

    a. Retention Assets. Naval ships withdrawn from service by MSC for inactivation and designated as OSIR retention assets will normally be laid up in the Navy's inactive ship inventory per a COMNAVSEASYSCOM INACTSHIPOFF inactivation plan. If an MSC OSIR retention asset is laid up in a MARAD NDRF facility, MARAD's reserve fleet manual safe stowage requirements apply and COMNAVSEASYSCOM INACTSHIPOFF shall be responsible for monitoring and continuing readiness of these ships.

    b. Disposal Assets. When an MSC ship is designated for disposal upon inactivation, MSC ships will first be offered to MARAD for title transfer. When MARAD accepts, the method of inactivation shall be per MARAD's MA-496 safe stowage requirements and towed directly to an NDRF facility upon completion of MSC inactivation. COMNAVSEASYSCOM will coordinate with MSC to tow such ships directly to an NDRF facility.

    c. Funding. Responsibilities for the inactivation of Navy ships under MSC command are found in chapter 9.

7. <u>Funding for Navy-owned Ships in the NDRF</u>. The ship's OPNAV ship resource and platform sponsor, via the cognizant customer BSO, is responsible for funding the inactivation work and the cost for first year lay-up of a vessel at MARAD. The inactivation work can be funded from the applicable appropriation per fiscal policy. All retention costs shall be funded from the 2B2G budget line.

CHAPTER 14
TRAINING POLICY

1. General

a. Upon inactivation of a ship or class of ships, the appropriate training support must be reviewed for applicability to other classes of ships. A determination must be made regarding continuation of training as the ships are decommissioned. If training involves inter-Service training organization (ITRO) courses, adherence to ITRO regulations should be considered.

b. The Naval Education and Training Security Assistance Field Activity (NETSAFA), in cooperation with COMNAVSEASYSCOM, will conduct a review of those courses and training pipelines that support a particular class of ships or individual systems aboard ships to determine the necessity of maintaining the training, in support of potential reactivation of retention assets or in support of FMS programs.

2. Disposition of Training Courses. In the event training is no longer required, the courses are to be disestablished and resources reprogrammed.

a. Course material, technical training equipment, and training devices that support ships retained as mobilization assets will be placed in storage by NETSAFA until the ship or last ship of the class is stricken; unless NETSAFA determines that there are less costly training alternatives available in the event of mobilization. In the event reactivation of mobilization assets is ordered, courses are to be reestablished as approved by CNO based on the recommendation of NETSAFA, the TYCOM, COMNAVSEASYSCOM, and Naval Education and Training Command (NETC). Additionally courses must be reviewed to ensure other ships are not affected by deactivation of training.

b. Once the last ship of a class is stricken, COMNAVSEASYSCOM, in coordination with NETC, resource and platform sponsors, and TYCOMs, will develop and execute a ship class training transition plan that identifies the most cost-effective training method and a timeline for transitioning the training execution from NETC to COMNAVSEASYSCOM. Upon transition of training execution from NETC to COMNAVSEASYSCOM, course material, technical training equipment, and training devices will be transferred to NETSAFA.

c.   During negotiations for the transfer of ships to other government agencies or foreign nations, a determination will be made as to whether U.S. Navy training support will be included with the transfer of the ship. Courses that support systems aboard ships that were transferred to other government agencies or foreign nations will not be discontinued until final disposition is determined by NETSAFA.

d.   Instructors and support staff for discontinued training will be reassigned based on NETC recommendation to Chief of Naval Personnel.

APPENDIX A
DEFINITIONS AND ACRONYMS

1. <u>Active Status</u>. Active status ships or service craft are assigned to the active fleets and to their supporting activities or are ships of MSC, which are titled in the United States or are operated under long-term bareboat charter. Ships and service craft in active status are "in commission" or "in service."

2. <u>Battle Force Ships</u>. Includes aircraft carriers, surface combatants, submarines, amphibious warfare ships, mine warfare ships, MSC's combat logistic force, and fleet support ships in an active status, per reference (l).

3. <u>Cannibalization</u>. Equipment or parts removal for reutilization in response to a request to satisfy Navy CASREP when such parts are not available for drawdown from the supply system. The act of removing serviceable parts from one item of equipment in order to install them on another item of equipment.

4. <u>Cold Ship Transfer</u>. Transfer of title for an inactive ship in storage to a Federal, State, local government, or non-government agency or foreign government from the U.S. Navy.

5. <u>Custodian</u>. Organization responsible for the safe storage of decommissioned and inactive vessels that are either awaiting disposal or are to be retained as defined by this instruction. Custodial responsibilities are normally assigned by CNO to COMNAVSEASYSCOM or a fleet commander and are then further delegated to a COMNAVSEASYSCOM INACTSHIPOFF or a TYCOM.

6. <u>Decommission</u>. Removal of a commissioned U.S. Navy ship from active status.

7. <u>Decommissioning Ceremony</u>. A ceremony that signifies the official retirement of a ship and honors all of the men and women who gave their time, energy, and, for some, their lives while serving aboard. The decommissioning ceremony does not have to occur coincident to the decommissioning date.

8. <u>Decommissioning Date</u>. The date the vessel is no longer considered a commissioned vessel. Transfer of command paperwork is signed and legal authority and liability is surrendered by the ship's CO.

9. <u>Dismantlement</u>. Also referred to as scrapping. The breakdown, abatement, and recycling of a ship.

10. <u>Equipage</u>. An item that requires management control afloat due to high unit cost, vulnerability to pilferage, and or being essential to the ship's mission. It does not encompass installed mechanical, electrical, ordnance, or electronic components or systems. The allowed quantity of equipage items is determined on an individual ship basis. Examples include: lines, firearms, anchor chain, gas masks, copy machines, etc.

11. <u>Equipment</u>. Any functional unit of hull, mechanical, electrical, ordnance, or electronic type material that is identified by a component identification number, numerical control code, allowance parts list, or similar designation, or is operated as a component of a system or subsystem. Examples include: pumps, radars, guns, ovens, etc.

12. <u>Equipment Removal</u>. Removal from a ship, incident to its inactivation or its disposal, of installed equipment, on-board allowances of spares, repair parts, consumable material, technical manuals, etc., for which there is a requirement.

13. <u>Excess</u>. Any property under the control of any Federal agency that is not required for its needs and the discharge of its responsibility.

14. <u>Expected Service Life (ESL)</u>. The number of years a naval ship is expected to be in service.

15. <u>Experimental Use</u>. Utilization of an inactive naval vessel for research and development, or an acquisition program.

16. <u>Fleet Commanders</u>. COMUSFLTFORCOM and COMPACFLT are the Navy's fleet commanders. They are the echelon 2, naval service component commanders responsible for executing reference (b) responsibilities for manning, training, maintaining, and equipping naval forces to support combatant commander and naval component commander requirements.

17. <u>Fleet Training Exercise</u>. A Navy exercise involving an inactive vessel which is conducted under such conditions that the vessel is likely to sink or is deliberately sunk for the purpose of training personnel, testing weapons, or studying the survivability of ship structures.

18. <u>Hot Ship Transfer</u>. Transfer of ship's custody from the U.S. Navy to a Federal, State, or local government, non-government agency, or foreign government coincident with the ship's official retirement.

19. <u>Inactivation</u>. The process by which a ship is prepared for retirement.

20. <u>Inactive Ship Inventory</u>. The total population of inactive ships and service craft that have been retired and are under the custody or responsibility of COMNAVSEASYSCOM's Navy Inactive Ships Program.

21. <u>Inactive Status</u>. Ships and service craft that are in reserve and not currently required for duty in the active fleets or supporting forces.

22. <u>Inactive Vessel</u>. Any ship or service craft that has been retired from active service.

23. <u>Inactivation Availability</u>. Period of time after a ship shifts from operational status, prior to its official retirement, during which the inactivation process normally commences.

24. <u>Insurance Items</u>. Systems, equipment, or major components required to replace damaged installations when such installed items cannot be readily repaired, or when a replacement procured due to extended repair or acquisition lead time. These items do not have an anticipated demand which justifies system stock.

25. <u>Logistic Support Asset</u>. An inactivated vessel utilized as a primary means of cannibalization and equipment removal for ships. Cannibalizations and equipment removal from such vessels is authorized without replacement.

26. <u>Maintenance Categories</u>. Indicates the priority sequence for the level of maintenance to be accomplished.

27. <u>Maritime Administration (MARAD)</u>. An agency of the U.S. Department of Transportation responsible for the NDRF and the RRF.

28. <u>Material Inspection</u>. A periodic inspection conducted to ascertain and report to Congress on the material condition and performance capabilities or limitations of Navy ships and submarines as defined by the Board of INSURV, per references (f) and (g).

29. <u>Merchant Convertible</u>. A vessel that can be modified for economically viable merchant use, as determined by MARAD.

30. <u>Naval Vessel Register</u>. A listing of ships and service craft that comprise the official inventory of the U.S. Navy.

31. <u>Operational Commander</u>. Organizational authority responsible for effectively using available resources and for planning the employment of, organizing, directing, coordinating and controlling military forces for the accomplishment of assigned missions.

32. <u>Office of the Chief of Naval Operations (OPNAV)</u>. The CNO is the principal advisor and naval executive to SECNAV on the conduct of naval activities of the DON. Assistants are the Vice Chief of Naval Operations, the DCNOs, and a number of other ranking officers. These officers and their staffs are collectively known as the "Office of the Chief of Naval Operations."

33. <u>OPNAV Ship Resource and Platform Sponsor</u>. Organization within OPNAV responsible for specific ship types in fulfillment of assigned warfare requirements and programs.

34. <u>Out of Commission, In Reserve (OCIR)</u>. Status of a decommissioned Navy ship being held in reserve for future mobilization purposes.

35. <u>Out of Service, In Reserve (OSIR)</u>. Status of a non-commissioned Navy vessel being held in reserve for future mobilization purposes.

36. <u>Out of Service</u>. Term used for Navy service craft and non-commissioned ships removed from use by the U.S. Navy.

37. <u>Payback</u>. A replacement of equipment or part removed that is equivalent in form, fit, function, and material condition to the equipment or part removed, so that interoperability of the payback is assured if the ship has to be reactivated. Typically applies to those vessels being retained for future mobilization purposes, foreign military transfer, and as potential memorial and museum assets.

38. <u>Retention Asset</u>. A vessel designated as a potential future mobilization asset.

39. <u>Retirement</u>. The transitioning of a naval ship or craft from active to inactive status by decommissioning or placing out of service.

40. <u>Service Craft</u>. A classification of waterborne craft which comprises the waterborne utilitarian craft not classified as ships or boats, designed to operate in coastal and protected waters, and provide general support to combatant forces and shore establishments. Service craft are designated by type in reference (l), and listed in the Craft and Boat Support System and the Naval Vessel Register. This definition is per reference (a).

41. <u>Ships</u>. A classification of water-borne craft which comprises the oceangoing vessels and craft of the Navy, and such other water-borne craft as may be assigned this classification.

42. <u>Special Status</u>. Ships and service craft in special status shall include those units for which the Navy is charged with certain responsibilities by reason of custody or title, but which are not in a commissioned or in-Service status. Ships and service craft in special status are "out of commission, special," or "out of service, special."

43. <u>Strike</u>. The declaration by SECNAV or designee that a ship or service craft be removed from the Naval Vessel Register.

44. <u>Survey</u>. Any inspection conducted to document the material condition of a ship prior to inactivating.

45. <u>Target Exercise</u>. A Navy exercise with a vessel, conducted on a not-to-sink basis, for the purpose of training personnel, testing weapons, or studying the survivability of ship structures.

46. <u>Type Commander (TYCOM)</u>. A member of the COMUSFLTFORCOM or COMPACFLT responsible for supervising personnel, training, logistics, maintenance, and other support to naval ships and units for air, surface, and submarines.

47. <u>Vessel</u>. Includes every description of watercraft or other artificial contrivance used, or capable of being used, as a means of transportation on water.

Acronyms

ADCON	administrative control
ASN (RD&A)	Assistant Secretary of the Navy for Research, Development, and Acquisition
BSO	budget submitting office
C4I	command, control, communications, computers, and intelligence
CASREP	casualty report
CNO	Chief of Naval Operations
CO	commanding officer
COMNAVAIRLANT	Commander, Naval Air Forces Atlantic
COMNAVAIRPAC	Commander, Naval Air Forces Pacific
COMNAVAIRSYSCOM	Commander, Naval Air Systems Command
COMNAVSEASYSCOM	Commander, Naval Sea Systems Command
COMSUBFOR	Commander, Submarine Forces
COMSUBPAC	Commander, Submarine Forces, Pacific
COMNAVSUPSYSCOM	Commander, Naval Supply Systems Command
COMNAVSURFLANT	Commander, Naval Surface Forces, Atlantic
COMNAVSURFPAC	Commander, Naval Surface Forces, Pacific
COMPACFLT	Commander, U.S. Pacific Fleet
COMSPAWARSYSCOM	Commander, Space and Naval Warfare Systems Command
COMUSFLTFORCOM	Commander, U.S. Fleet Forces Command
DASN	Deputy Assistant Secretary of the Navy
DCNO	Deputy Chief of Naval Operations
DNS	Director, Navy Staff
DoD	Department of Defense
DON	Department of the Navy
DRMO	Defense Reutilization and Marketing Office
ECDIS-N	Electronic Charting Display Information System-Navy
EPA	Environmental Protection Agency
ERS	Equipment Removal System
ESL	expected service life
FDNF	forward-deployed naval force
FMB	Department of the Navy, Office of Financial Management and Budget
FMS	foreign military sales
FY	fiscal year
FYDP	Future Years Defense Program
IM	inventory manager
INACTSHIPMAINTO	Inactive Ships On-site Maintenance Office
INACTSHIPOFF	Inactive Ships Management Office

INSURV	Board of Inspection and Survey
ISEA	in-service engineering agent or activity
ITRO	inter-Service training organization
LOA	letter of offer and acceptance
MAM	maintenance assist modules
MARAD	Maritime Administration
MSC	Military Sealift Command
NAVSUPSYSCOM	Naval Supply Systems Command
Navy IPO	Navy International Programs Office
NDRF	National Defense Reserve Fleet
NETC	Naval Education and Training Command
NETSAFA	Naval Education and Training Security Assistance Field Activity
NRF	Navy Reserve Force
NTCSS	Navy Tactical Command Support System
OCIR	out of commission, in reserve
OPCON	operational control
OPNAV	Office of the Chief of Naval Operations
OSIR	out of service, in reserve
POM	program objective memorandum
PPBE	Planning, Programming, Budgeting and Execution
RRF	Ready Reserve Force
SDR	Ship Disposition Review
SECNAV	Secretary of the Navy
SID	Ship Inactivation Decision
SYSCOM	systems command
TYCOM	type commander
USCG	United States Coast Guard
USMC	United States Marine Corps
USNS	United States Naval Ship

APPENDIX B
EQUIPMENT REMOVAL DURING DECOMMISSIONING INACTIVATION

Type of Material	TYPE OF SHIP DISPOSITION						
	RETENTION	NON-RETENTION					
	Mobilization	Logistic Support Asset	FMS Hot Transfer	FMS Cold Transfer	Donation	Target & Experimental Use	Dismantlement & Title Transfer
Bench stocks	C	C	D	D	C	C	C
Storeroom consumables	C	C	D	D	C	C	C
All repair parts, spares, and MAM	A	C	D	D	C	C	C
Installed Combat Systems	C	C	F	F	C	C	C
Installed C4I Systems	C	C	F	F	C	C	C
Installed H&ME Systems	A	C	F	F	C	C	C
Test equipment	A	C	D	D	C	C	D
Item manager controlled equipment	B	B	D	D	B	B	B
Medical/dental supplies	C	C	D	D	C	C	C
Curator interest items	C	C	C	C	C	C	C
Welfare and Recreation equipment	C	C	C	C	C	C	C
Cash registers	C	C	C	C	C	C	C
Merchandise in ship's store and in clothing and small stores	C	C	C	C	C	C	C
Resale system-owned equipment	B	B	B	B	B	B	B
Radiac equipment	B	B	B	B	B	B	B
Biological warfare and or chemical warfare protective clothing	B	B	B	B	B	B	B
Chemical and biological agent detection equipment	B	B	B	B	B	B	B
Dosimeters	B	B	B	B	B	B	B
Night vision devices	C	C	C	C	C	C	C
Non-commercial satellite communication equipment	B	B	B	B	B	B	B
Special purpose test equipment for electronic equipment that will not transfer with the vessel	C	C	C	C	C	C	C
Sonobuoys and sonobuoy data links	B	B	B	B	B	B	B
Micro-miniature repair stations	C	C	C	C	C	C	C
Field calibration equipment	C	C	C	C	C	C	C
Standard Network Access Protocol and Navy Tactical Command Support System (NTCSS) systems and software	B	B	B	B	B	B	B
Site television system	B	B	B	B	B	B	B
Record message traffic processing equipment	B	B	B	B	B	B	B
Material that provides low observable capability	B	B	B	B	B	B	B
All biometric collection equipment and its peripherals	B	B	B	B	B	B	B
All body armor systems	C	C	C	C	C	C	C
Laser range finders	C	C	C	C	C	C	C
Non-lethal weapons	C	C	C	C	C	C	C

Note: This table is provided for planning purposes. For specific guidance on disposition of other than installed equipment for FMS transfers, see reference (i). Additional guidance on the removal of equipment from inactivating ships can be found in chapter 12.

1. A - Retain aboard (except for non-transferable technology items on vessels designated for foreign transfer). Special consideration shall be given to ensure that non-transferable technology is removed or sanitized prior to inactivation.

2. B - Offload for return to supply system or IM. Except for FMS hold ships, excess material not required by the supply system or IM will be offloaded to the Defense Reutilization and Marketing Office (DRMO). NTCSS equipment is redistributed by COMSPAWARSYSCOM Headquarters.

3. C - TYCOM redistributes; remaining material shall be offloaded for return to supply system. Excess material not required by the supply system will be offloaded to DRMO. All general use items may be removed and redistributed. For curator interest items, TYCOM will comply with chapter 11. For mobilization assets, COMNAVSEASYSCOM shall be responsible for subsequent payback if the vessel is mobilized.

4. D - See reference (i) for specific guidance on ships designated for foreign military transfer.

5. E - Life cycle IMs will determine if items are required to fill insurance item inventory shortfalls and take actions to remove if needed.

6. F - OPNAV N9I retains discretion as to the disposition. Guidance will be issued on a case-by-case basis. See chapter 6 for specific guidance.

APPENDIX C
CONVENTIONAL SHIP INACTIVATION TIMELINE

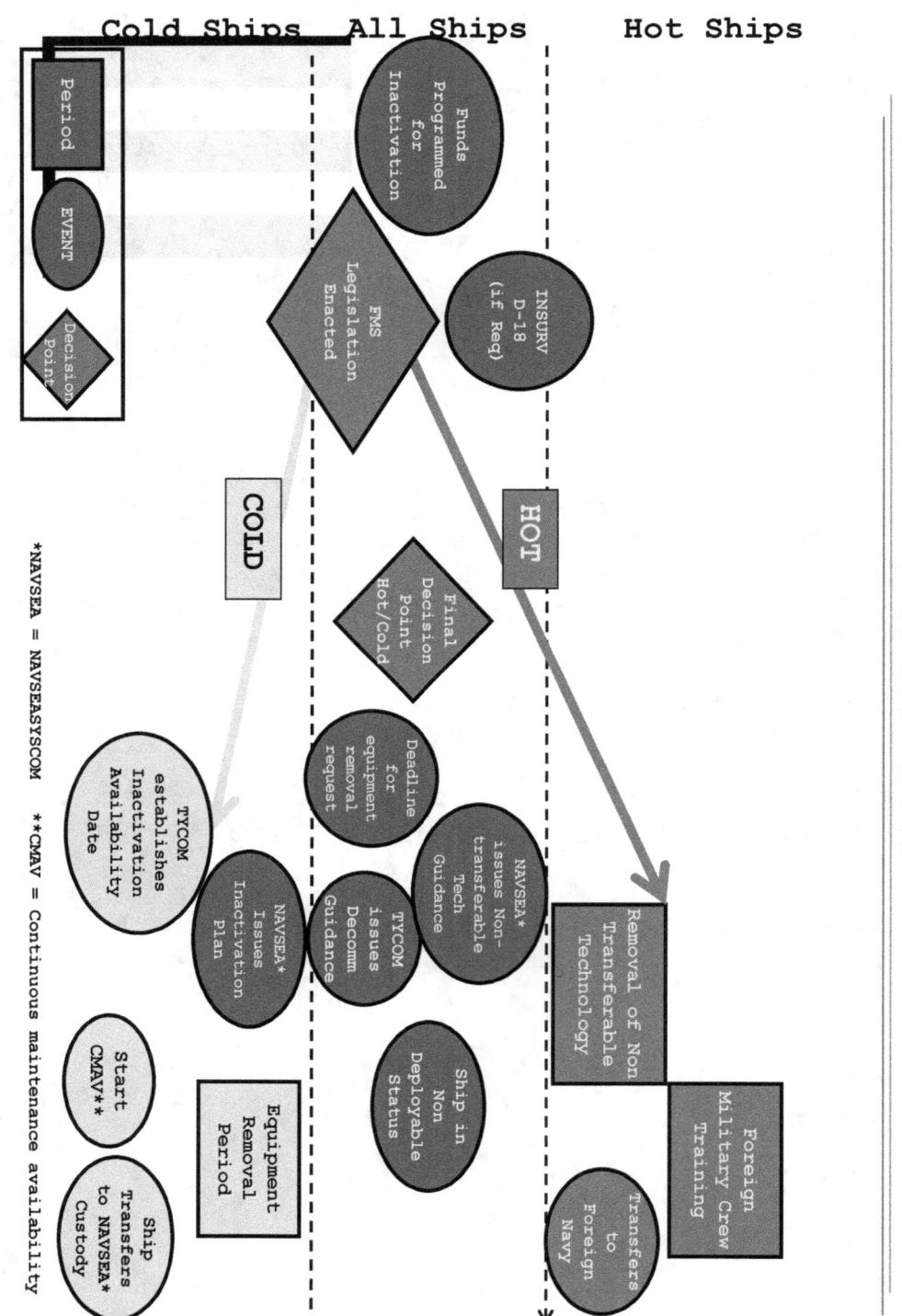

APPENDIX D
NAVAL VESSEL LIFE CYCLE

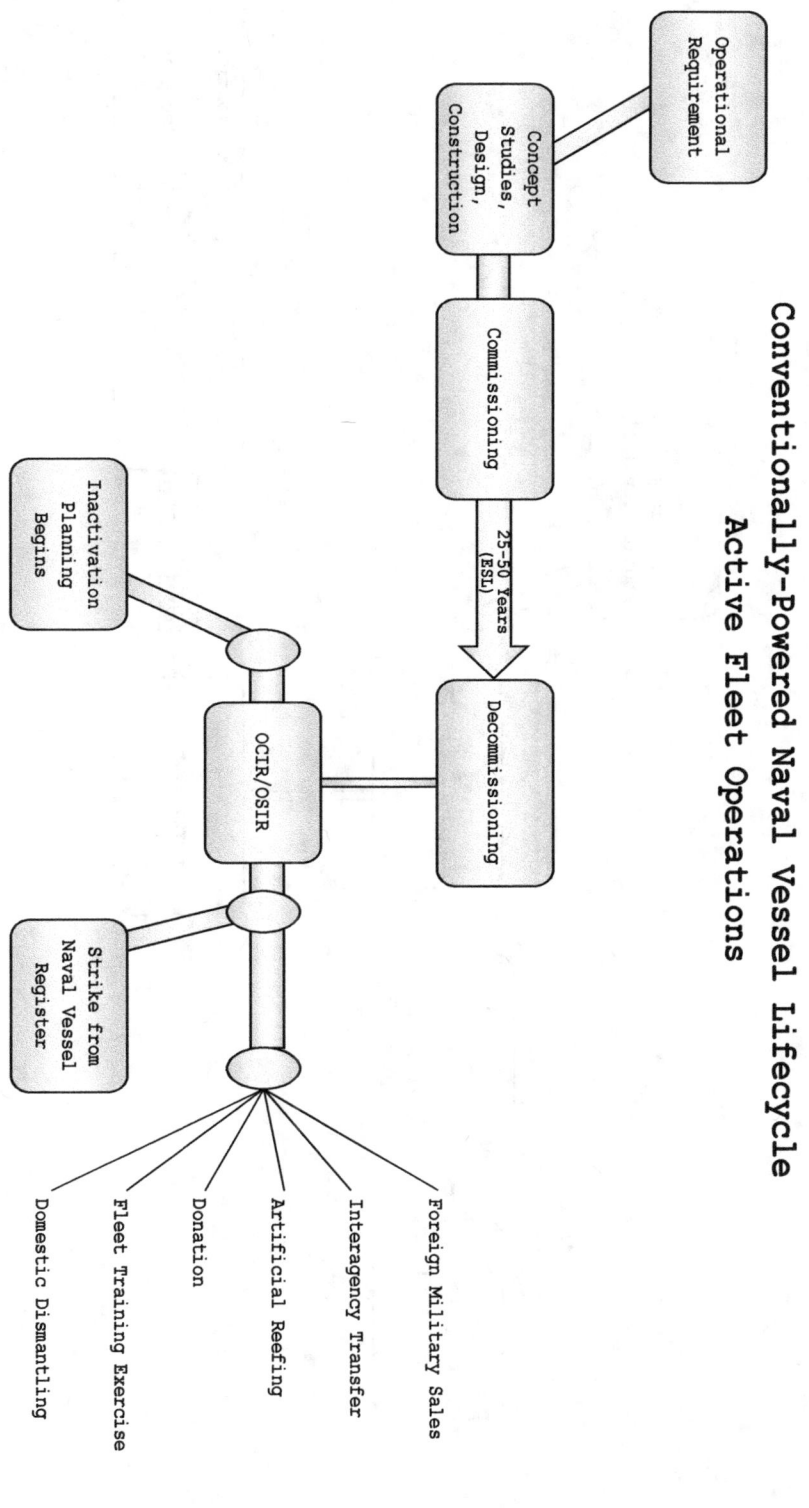

Conventionally-Powered Naval Vessel Lifecycle
Active Fleet Operations

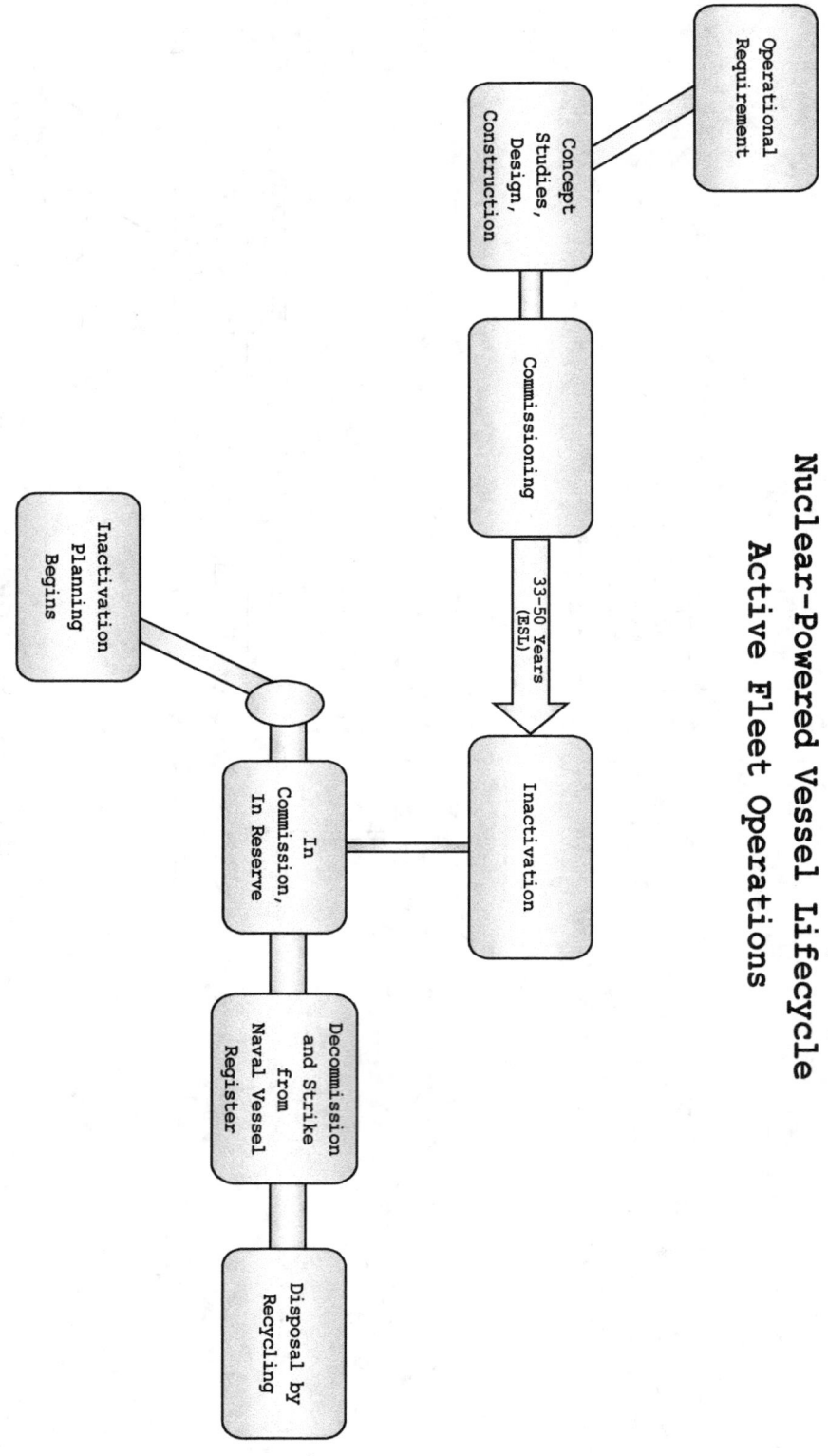

OPNAVINST 4770.5H
24 Apr 2014

Nuclear-Powered Vessel Lifecycle
Active Fleet Operations

Operational Requirement → **Concept Studies, Design, Construction** → **Commissioning** → (33-50 Years (ESL)) → **Inactivation** → **In Commission, In Reserve** ← **Inactivation Planning Begins**; **In Commission, In Reserve** → **Decommission and Strike from Naval Vessel Register** → **Disposal by Recycling**

D-2

APPENDIX E
SHIP DISPOSITION DECISION FLOW CHART

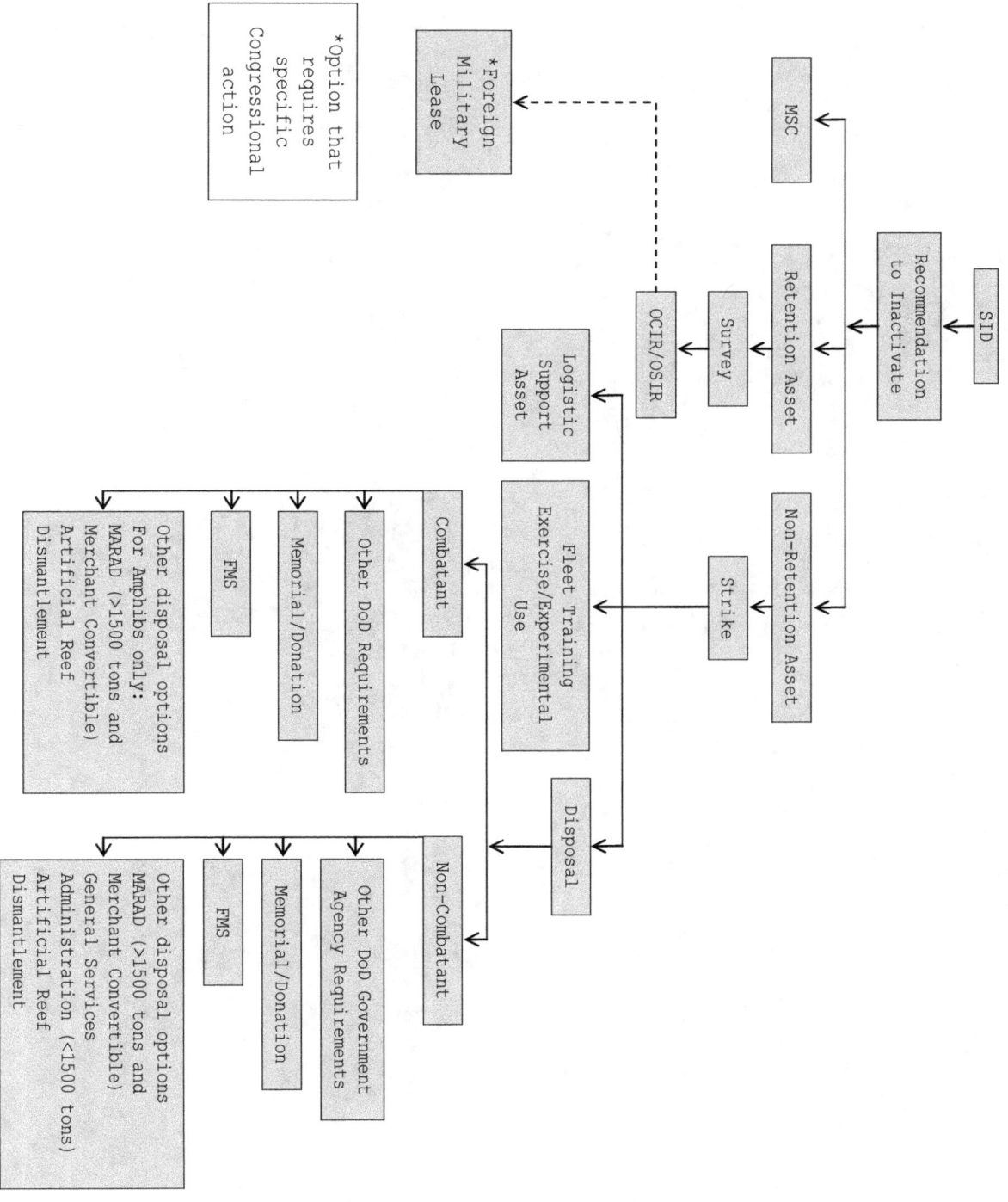

www.ingramcontent.com/pod-product-compliance
Lightning Source LLC
Chambersburg PA
CBHW081407280526
45788CB00009B/3013